本教材为2021年教育部"新文科"建设专项项目阶段性成果
项目名称:"新文科"背景下行业特色高校外语专业优化研究与实践
项目编号:2021050084

语言学入门

Essentials for Classical General Linguistics

主　编　林　忠
副主编　王　凤　刘存伟

西安交通大学出版社　国家一级出版社
XI'AN JIAOTONG UNIVERSITY PRESS　全国百佳图书出版单位

图书在版编目（CIP）数据

语言学入门：Essentials for Classical General Linguistics：汉文、英文/林忠主编.
—西安：西安交通大学出版社，2021.12（2022.8重印）
　ISBN 978-7-5693-2329-0

　Ⅰ.①语… Ⅱ.①林… Ⅲ.①语言学—汉、英 Ⅳ.①H0

中国版本图书馆CIP数据核字(2021)第212215号

语言学入门
Essentials for Classical General Linguistics

主　　编	林　忠
责任编辑	蔡乐芊
责任校对	李　蕊
装帧设计	伍　胜

出版发行	西安交通大学出版社
	（西安市兴庆南路1号　邮政编码710048）
网　　址	http://www.xjtupress.com
电　　话	（029）82668357　82667874（市场营销中心）
	（029）82668315（总编办）
传　　真	（029）82668280
印　　刷	西安日报社印务中心

开　　本	710 mm×1000 mm　1/16　印张　13.875　字数　326千字
版次印次	2021年12月第1版　2022年8月第2次印刷
书　　号	ISBN 978-7-5693-2329-0
定　　价	55.00元

如发现印装质量问题，请与本社市场营销中心联系。
订购热线：（029）82665248　（029）82667874
投稿热线：（029）82665371
读者信箱：xjtu_rw@163.com

版权所有　侵权必究

编委会

主　编　林忠（长安大学）
副主编　王凤（西安电子科技大学）
　　　　刘存伟（重庆邮电大学）
编　者　刘宇（长安大学）
　　　　贾艳萍（长安大学）
　　　　潘立慧（广西大学）
　　　　林竞（厦门理工学院）
　　　　刘士川（四川文理学院）
　　　　李显文（四川文理学院）
　　　　李长安（盐城工学院）
　　　　王士齐（华东师范大学）
　　　　廉虹（西安电子科技大学）
　　　　姜宁（西安电子科技大学）
　　　　郭菁文（布里斯托大学）
　　　　潘丽红（利兹大学）

前　　言

　　语言是人类思想的载体，也是组成人类社会的重要部分。语言学课程可以帮助学生了解语言与经济、文化、科技等的关系，提高语言艺术修养，提升语言运用能力，发展理性思维，拓宽国际视野。本教材编写组秉持课程思政理念，依据教育部《普通高等学校本科专业类教学质量国家标准（外国语言文学类）》《高等学校课程思政建设指导纲要》及《普通高等学校本科外国语言文学类专业教学指南（2020）》等文件的精神，编写了《语言学入门》这本教材。

　　本教材力求搭建系统的普通语言学基础理论框架，探究语言本质、起源和发展。教材内容深入浅出，力求消除学生对语言学的畏难心理，培养学生对语言学分支学科的兴趣，形成知识探究与创新能力，引导学生树立健全的人格品质和正确的价值取向。本教材的编写遵循以下几个原则：

　　一、坚持课程思政精神，思政元素与教材内容相互融合，真正实现培根铸魂，启智增慧。传统的语言学教材主要围绕语言学的基础理论知识展开，而在课程思政精神的号召下，我们希望将文化、社会、科学融入语言学教材中，在传授语言学知识的同时，提升学生的道德素养，培养家国情怀，增强民族自信心。我们希望，这些思政元素的融入可以帮助学生将繁杂深奥的语言学理论剥茧抽丝，在实践中学会思辨，提升整体素养。比如，我们在教材中设计了"学术规范资源"版块，力求提升学生信息素养，增强其学术道德感，引导学生加强对学术规范的科学认知，合理使用学术研究工具；设计"中华语言文化鉴赏与思考"版块，寓中华文化于语言学知识中，在知识中提炼中华语言文化价值，帮助学生建立语言、文化自信。这些设计都是践行立德树人培养目标的具体体现。

二、本教材包含经典普通语言学的基础理论，重点突出，能帮助学生在把握每章节内容全貌的同时拥有自主学习和探索的空间。章节设置按普通语言学分支结构划分，共分为七个章节，包括语言学概述、语音、音位、形态、句法、语义，以及语用。第一章为概述，对语言及现代语言学的概貌进行讲解。学生将在第一章的学习中，了解什么是语言和语言学。第二章对语音学中的音素、发声器官，以及英语元音、辅音音标的不同分类，以及划分标准进行系统的介绍。通过第二章的学习，学生能够站在语音学家研究声音的角度，了解声音是如何发出并被学习和研究的，同时了解人们是如何使用国际音标字母表（IPA）来标记与指代不同语言的各种声音的。第三章着重介绍音位学，包括音素、同位音素等概念，以及语音系统中的语音规则、重音、语调等理论。第四章涵盖形态学的重点内容，学生将从语素着手，学习语素的划分，以及不同类别语素组成单词的规则等内容。第五章包含句法、句子成分，以及句子结构等方面的内容。第六章集中解释自然语言中不同语言单位的语义关系等理论。第七章涉及语用学中的重点理论，对言语行为、言语行为理论、会话规则等内容进行了讲解。

三、教材内容取材广泛，参考、吸纳国内外语言学教材精华，包括 Charles W. Kredler 的 *Introducing English Semantics*，Peter Ladefoged 与 Keith Johnson 的 *A Course in Phonetics*，John McWhorter 的 *Understanding Linguistics: The Science of Language* 等。全书删繁就简，呈现出专业、科学的基本语言学理论内容；在内容设计上体现交融性、动态性与连贯性；在配套资源上结合多介质素材，提供包括多媒体课件、互联网资源，以及配套移动软件等在内的多介质教材资源。

四、教材内容设计体现"以学生为主体"的教育理念。在每个章节后设置了"自学活动与练习"及"章节框架"。"自学活动与练习"版块旨在培养学生的自主学习能力和实践能力。学生通过自主阅读完成相关概念检测题目，围绕语言学知识点，自发进行讨论和研究。在自主学习过程中，学生可以进一步巩固所学的理论知识，提高自己发现问题、分析问题、解决问题的能力。"章节框架"旨在帮助学生梳理理论内容，完成课后巩固以及考前复习回顾。在学习的每个阶段，学生均可对标大纲要求，检测学习目标的达成情况，从而检验学习效果。

我们希望《语言学入门》能够引导学生进入语言学的大门，了解语言学诸多分支学科。同时，希望本教材能够为新文科建设、外语学科改革和发展，以及课程思政贡献绵薄之力。本教材适合高校英语专业高年级本科生，也适合具有同等水平的学生进行自主学习。本教材的内容设计具有实用性和灵活性，授课教师可以根据学生的语言知识和能力，以及学校教学资源，选择书中多介质教材资源，进行线上或线下课程"实质等效"的讲解。由于编写时间紧迫，书中内容难免有疏漏，敬请读者批评指正。

编　者

Preface

Essentials for Classical General Linguistics is a coursebook specifically designed for an introductory course of linguistics that merges the cultivation of moral integrity and ideological education into curriculum. It covers the core areas of linguistics: phonetics, phonology, morphology, syntax, semantics, and pragmatics. It also contains various types of materials and activities to foster academic and moral development of college students. This book is compiled by the teachers from School of Foreign Studies of Chang'an University. We aim to provide a concise coursebook for the students who are just beginning to learn linguistics, a textbook covering the essentials in general linguistics without excessive complicated details and a textbook broadening students' academic knowledge as well as guiding their civic perceptions and morality in the new era.

First, *Essentials for Classical General Linguistics* is organised in a hierarchical way, starting from the smallest unit of the phonemes and then moving progressively to the biggest unit of language.

To provide a bottom-up description of English linguistics, the book is divided into seven chapters. Chapter 1 is an introductory section which provides a broad overview of English linguistics, answering such questions: *What is language? What is Linguistics? What are sub-fields of linguistics?* Chapter 2 discusses the sound system, presenting a description of speech organs and English sounds (vowels and consonants), introducing how English sounds are studied by phonetists and how people use the International Phonetic Alphabet (IPA) to indicate sounds in different languages. Chapter 3 shows the explicit discussion of speech segments (phonemes and allophones), phonological rules and suprasegmentals (syllables, stress and intonation). Chapter 4 describes the division of morphemes, the smallest unit of meaning, and how they are combined to create words. Chapter 5 presents the major syntactic categories in

English (words, phrases, clauses and sentences), and how they are constructed in sentences. Chapter 6 gives an introduction of how the meanings of words are described and how they are related, which is restricted to lexical semantics. Chapter 7 examines the language in the social aspect, including the ways meaning and action are related to language (Speech Act Theory), and some conversational rules.

Second, this book presents theoretical concepts in ways that capture the interest of students and motivate them to study linguistics in more depth. It refers to several foundational linguistics books by renowned linguists, like Charles F. Meyer's *Introducing English Linguistics,* Charles W. Kreidler's *Introducing English Semantics,* Peter Ladefoged and Keith Johnson's *A Course in Phonetics* and so on. Some important concepts and theories in these books are selected, extracted and weaved in the corresponding chapter of this book in the hope of introducing to students the basic theories of general linguistics instead of an overly theoretical framework. In each chapter, there is a special section of Further Reading, which is designed to enrich learners' understanding of linguistics and allow them to explore linguistics fields further.

Third, this book not only informs students of general linguistic knowledge, but also develops their social values and ideological consciousness by designing appropriate contents, exercises and activities to scaffold students' learning in practice. For example, the section of Linguistics and Life in each chapter helps students review linguistics from the Marxism perspectives. It includes reading texts and some critical thinking questions, so students are able to connect the language studies with their own life. The exercises in this book are selected from *Hello China* and other traditional Chinese literature such as *Analects of Confucius, Romance of the Three Kingdoms* and so on, which aim to enhance students' understanding of the main linguistic concepts as well as nurture students' morality.

Fourth, this book is student-friendly in use. At the end of each chapter, there is an outline which helps students review the contents of this course, understand relationships among different elements, and prepare for assessments. Learning and research recourses are provided including many research tools, international journals and academic learning sites. Students can make use of these resources to explore the research front and develop their academic interests in different topics. Meanwhile, students can enhance their problem-solving abilities in the process of searching information and finding the answers on their own from such resources.

Essentials for Classical General Linguistics can be used as a textbook for an introductory course of linguistics. As a textbook for an undergraduate readership, it presupposes that students have little or no background in learning linguistics, so it incorporates and discusses basic linguistic terms and global theoretical framework. All essential technical terminologies are in bold print when they first appear. The glossary provides clear definitions of terminology.

Finally, we would like to express our thanks to all those who helped us directly or indirectly in editing *Essentials for Classical General Linguistics*. Linguistics is the scientific study of language, and learning linguistics can help students learn the language in a volume of larger dimensions. This book will, we hope, be of use to lead all learners through the study of general linguistics. We also welcome comments and feedback on all aspects of this book.

目 录

1 **Introduction** 1
   1.1 What Is Linguistics? 1
   1.2 Descriptivism vs Prescriptivism 2
   1.3 What Is Language? 2
   1.4 Language and Speech 3
   1.5 Language and Medium 3
   1.6 Two-Part Structure of Sign Systems 4
   1.7 Three Substructures of Language 4
   1.8 What Is Grammar? 7
   Summary 9
   Self-Study Activities 12
   Further Reading 13
   Outline 13

2 **Phonetics** 16
   2.1 Introduction 16
   2.2 Speech Organs 17
   2.3 Sounds of Language 18
   2.4 Vowels 27
   2.5 Sounds beyond Those in English 30

Summary 33

Self-Study Activities 35

Further Reading 37

Outline 37

3 Phonology 40

3.1 Introduction 40

3.2 Speech Segments 40

3.3 Allophones 42

3.4 Phonological Rules 44

3.5 Suprasegmentals 54

Summary 62

Self-Study Activities 63

Further Reading 64

Outline 64

4 Morphology 67

4.1 Introduction 67

4.2 Morphemes 67

4.3 Morphological Processes: Inflection and Derivation ... 73

4.4 Compound Words 78

Summary 80

Self-Study Activities 84

Further Reading 85

Outline 85

5 Syntax ... 87
5.1 Introduction ... 87
5.2 Basic Syntactic Notions ... 89
5.3 Word Classes ... 92
5.4 Phrase ... 101
5.5 Clause ... 105
5.6 Sentence ... 108
5.7 Deep Structure and Surface Structure ... 114
Summary ... 116
Self-Study Activities ... 118
Further Reading ... 121
Outline ... 121

6 Semantics ... 124
6.1 Introduction ... 124
6.2 Semantic Roles ... 124
6.3 Semantic Relations ... 126
6.4 Figurative Language ... 133
Summary ... 140
Self-Study Activities ... 143
Further Reading ... 144
Outline ... 145

7 Pragmatics ... 148
7.1 Introduction ... 148

    7.2   Five Linguistic Situations Requiring Pragmatic Inference 150

    7.3   Speech Act Theory 158

    7.4   Cooperative Talk: Conversational Rules 161

    7.5   Syntax vs Semantics vs Pragmatics 166

    Summary 168

    Self-Study Activities 171

    Further Reading 172

    Outline 173

Glossary 175

Answers to Self-Study Activities 196

Bibliography 204

1 Introduction

People outside the field of linguistics are often unclear about what linguistics is. Linguistics is the scientific study of language, as opposed to understandable but impressionistic analyses of language. In this course, we will introduce students to modern linguistics and explain how linguists study language.

1.1 What Is Linguistics?

- **Linguistics is** usually defined as "the scientific study of language". The study of grammar has a long history and many of the ideas central to current linguistic theory can be traced back to ancient times.

- **Linguistics** is a discipline that concerns the study of all aspects of the present day, with a methodological outlook firmly based on the working practices and developed in modern contemporary linguistics.

The definition of linguistics as the scientific study of language raises two questions: what do we mean by "scientific" and what do we mean by "language"? The first one can be answered relatively easily, but the second needs to be examined more fully. When we say that a linguist aims to be scientific, we mean that he/she attempts to study language in much the same way as a scientist studies physics or chemistry, systematically and without prejudice as far as possible. It means observing language use, forming hypotheses about it, testing these hypotheses and refining them on the basis of the evidence collected.

Now, linguistics is firmly situated as its own field. Linguistics departments have emerged in universities around the world, increasing in size and number nearly every year. Linguistics is also found in other areas of study, including philosophy, anthropology, computer science, psychology, and speech pathology. Linguistics is becoming more and more central to the study of language and literature in English departments and to the study of language acquisition, learning, and teaching in modern languages departments (sometimes called foreign or world languages departments).

In this book, we will go through how language is studied by linguists, and compare different languages such as Chinese and English. In the following chapters, there are many examples shown in both English and Chinese.

1.2 Descriptivism vs Prescriptivism

Here we will discuss the difference between linguistic descriptivism and prescriptivism, and we agree that linguists are descriptivists. Many people are known as prescriptivists. They always tell you what is right and what is wrong, and that you should talk in this way or write in that way. In a word, they prescribe the precise way of speaking or writing. However, we would like to tell you that:

- Linguists are only concerned with describing the way language is ACTUALLY used by speech communities (and their underlying language systems).
- This contrasts with prescriptivism, which claims that there is a right or a wrong way to speak.

1.3 What Is Language?

- Language is what makes us human, and we all seem to be naturally curious about it.
- A language is a set of signals by which we communicate. There are a number of other general points that are worth making about language.

First, human language is not only a vocal system of communication. It can be expressed in writing, with the result that it is not limited in time or space. Second, each language is both arbitrary and systematic. By this we mean that no two languages are presented in exactly the same way, each with its own set of rules. And finally, there are no primitive or inferior languages. People may live in the most primitive conditions but all languages appear to be equally complex and all are absolutely adequate to the needs of their users.

1.4 Language and Speech

Language in the narrow sense is a system of means of expression, while **speech** should be understood as the manifestation of the system of language in the process of interaction.

The system of language includes, on the one hand, the units that constitute language sounds, morphemes, words, word-groups, on the other hand, the regularities or "rules" of the use of these units. Speech comprises both the act of producing utterances, and the utterances themselves, i.e. the text. Language and speech are inseparable; they form an organic unity together. As for grammar (the grammatical system), being an integral part of the lingual macrosystem, it dynamically connects language with speech, because it categorially determines the lingual process of utterance production.

1.5 Language and Medium

A language is an abstraction based on the linguistic behaviour of its users. It is not to be equated precisely with speech because no speaker has total mastery of the entire system or is capable of using the language adequately due to tiredness, illness or inattention. All normal children of all races learn to speak the language of their community, so speech has often been seen as the primary medium of language. Language can also be realised by writing. Although speech and writing have much in common, they are not to be equated or hierarchically ordered. Speech and writing are complementary and both are necessary in a technologically advanced society. We can sum up the relationship between language and its mediums in a diagram shown in Figure 1.1.

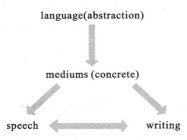

Figure 1.1　The relationship between language and its mediums.

The diagram indicates that, although speech and writing are in theory distinct, they do influence each other. A simple example of this is that pronunciation is often affected by spelling. A word like "often", for example, is not frequently pronounced with a "t" because of influence from the written medium.

1.6 Two-Part Structure of Sign Systems

Language is defined above as a sign system. Every sign system has two parts:

• **Lexicon**, or dictionary, the inventory of its signs,
• **Grammar**, the rules for the construction of its signs and for their combination into messages.

Consider an example of a very simple sign system, the traffic light. Its lexicon has three signs and, in one version, its grammar has three rules, as follows:

Lexicon:

Meanings	*Forms*
"stop"	red light
"go"	green light
"caution"	yellow light

Rules:
a. From top to bottom, the signs are ordered red, yellow, green.
b. One colour is lighted at a time.
c. The sequence of light is green, yellow, red, repeatedly.

Adding possibilities to the lexicon such as a flashing mode, or an arrow-shaped light, and possibilities to the rules such as simultaneous signs (green and yellow at the same time), increases the expressiveness and the complexity of the system. Finally, remember that a sign, or sign system, has a third component, the interpreter. Sign and sign systems are useless unless users have shared knowledge of them.

1.7 Three Substructures of Language

Within and cutting across this two-part structure of inventory and rules, language has three sorts of substructure: phonology, morphology, and syntax.

Phonology

Phonology concerns the sounds of language. A few languages that lack phonology are the manually signed languages of the deaf, which instead have parallel phonological rules which concern the sub-parts of the discrete gestures of hands.

Phonological form consists of phones, for example the phones [m], [æ] and [p] of *map*, and phones consist of even smaller units of phonological features, for example:

[labial], as presented at the start of the words *map*, *bad* and *wag*;
[voiced], as presented at the start of the words *bad* and *dad* and absent at the start of *pad* and *tad*;
[nasal], as presented at the first phone of *map* and the first and last phones of *name*.

These three features are simultaneously present in the phone [m], the first sound of *map*, the voiced labial nasal [m] (Phonetic writing is typically shown within square brackets, [ ].). Languages differ in the phonological features they employ, and in the possibilities for simultaneous or sequential co-occurrence of features.

The possibilities of combination or occurrence of phonological features in morphemes are expressed by phonological rules. In English, for example, the feature [nasal] is present in vowels which precede nasal consonants, as in the vowel for *pan* and *bin*. You can confirm this for yourself by comparing the vowel sounds of these two words with those of *pad* and *bid*, which lack the final nasal consonant.

Morphology

Morphology concerns the classes of morphemes, and their co-occurrence in sentences and combination as words. Among the English morphemes, for example, are the following four, whose elements of form are in square brackets [ ], and elements of meaning in braces, ( );

[dɒg], (noun, "dog", animate, non-human,...)
[go], (verb, "go", intransitive,...)
[z], (plural suffix of nouns)
[z], (present tense suffix of verbs with third-person singular subject)

Morphological rules express the possible combinations of morphemes as words. For example, the first and third morphemes above, [dɒg] and [z], combine according to rules of English to produce the word [dɒgz] *dogs*, and the second and fourth morphemes [go] and [z] combine to produce the present tense verb [goz] *goes*. Don't let English spelling mislead you; the last consonant is pronounced [z], not [s].

Other languages have different forms for similar meanings, for example, French *chien* "dog", and simple words for meanings which English expresses by combining words, for example Amharic *ayat* "grandparent". But all languages have the capability to express the meanings expressed in other languages. The meaning of Amharic *ayat* is realized in English through the combination of words grand + parent.

Syntax

Syntax concerns the combinations of words as phrases and phrases as sentences. Every language has words, which constitute phrases and sentences. The possibilities of combination are strictly limited, so every language has syntax, or sentence structure.

Words come in different types based upon their possibilities of combination with other words in sentences. These types are the parts of speech: noun, verb, adjective, etc. Nouns, for example (such as *circus*, *pajamas*, and *story*), combine with determiners (such as *the*, *these*, *my*) and adjectives (such as *big*, *red*, *extraordinary*) to make noun phrases, such as *the big circus*, *these red pajamas*, and *my extraordinary story*. Verbs combine with auxiliary verbs (such as *can*, *might*, *will*, and *have*) and adverbs (such as *always*, *then*, and *surely*) to make verb phrases, such as *has already eaten*, *will leave them*, and *surely can't go*.

Syntactic rules specify the possible combinations of words as phrases and as sentences of general types, such as affirmative and negative, statements, commands, questions. In English, for example, questions answerable by yes or no are typically realized by sentences in which a so-called "auxiliary" verb appears before the noun phrase subject of the sentence, as in these examples:

Statement	Yes/ No question
This is wild China.	Is this wild China?
Chinese are fond of curiously shaped rocks.	Are Chinese fond of curiously shaped rocks?

Other Types of Linguistics Structure

In addition to phonology, morphology, and syntax, other types of linguistic structure may be recognised: semantic structure, concerning word and sentence meaning and their interpretation; orthographic structure, concerning writing; pragmatics structure, concerning how we use language to get meanings beyond those given forms of language; and discourse structure, concerning how sentences are fitted into longer stretches of language, as in conversations and arguments.

1.8 What Is Grammar?

Grammar is the linguistic rule system that we use to produce and understand sentences. In particular, the ability to combine discrete units into larger units forms the foundation of what linguists call grammar. A grammar is a complex system of rules that govern how speakers organise sounds into words and words into sentences.

The grammar of a language can be divided into four components. Each component interacts with others, but each can also be studied on its own.

- Phonetics: the inventory of sounds in a language;
- Phonology: rules of how sounds are combined in a language;
- Morphology: rules of word formation in a language;
- Semantics: rules that govern how meaning is expressed by words and sentences in language.

First, let's look at phonetics and phonology. For example, the phonetic system of English has (basically) twelve vowels, and the Hawaiian system has five. Sounds are merged in Hawaiian so that all words end in vowels; while so many English words end in consonants. English and Hawaiian thus vary both phonetically and phonologically.

Turn to morphology. In English we form the past participle of many verbs by attaching the suffix *-ed* to the root. For example, we attach *-ed* to the root *learn* to derive *learned*. In German, on the other hand, the past participles of the verb *lernen* (to learn) is *gelernt*, where the prefix *ge-* and suffix *-t* are attached to the root, *lern*. Although both English and German have past participles, the two languages differ morphologically in the rules to form them.

Languages also differ syntactically in the ways words are arranged in the sentence. For example, in English colour adjectives precede the nouns they modify, as in *red skirt* or *black cat*. In French, on the contrary, colour adjectives follow the noun: such as *jupe rouge* (skirt red) and *chat noir* (cat black).

Finally, we also find that the vocabulary is semantically distinct. Kinship words can vary in all languages, often dramatically. For example, in English, the word *grandmother* refers to family members that are two generations distant, great-great- refers to four generations distant, and so on. Njamal, on the other hand, has a word for the aboriginal Australian language relatives that applies to any two relatively distant, *maili*. This word can, for example, refer to the father of a father (two generations earlier) or the sister of the son of a daughter of a wife (two generations later).

Learning and Research Resources

- **Linguistic Network**

https://www.linguisticsnetwork.com/the-basics-of-linguistic-research/

Linguistics Network is an academically sound, user-friendly, and interactive online resource for linguistics and language-related studies. It covers the content in the major areas of linguistics studies that correspond with materials presented in lectures and textbooks used at major universities.

- **All about Linguistics**

http://all-about-linguistics.group.shef.ac.uk/

All about Linguistics is a website designed by a team at University of Sheffield, and on it you can find more about linguistics—the scientific study of human language. You can also observe how linguists describe and analyse languages, how language is learned and used by speakers, the history of its study and more.

- *Still Alice* (Film)

http://all-about-linguistics.group.shef.ac.uk/

Dr. Alice Howland is a renowned linguistics professor happily married with her physician husband John and she's got three adult children. All that begins to change when she strangely starts to forget words and then more. When her doctor diagnoses her with early-onset Alzheimer's Disease, Alice and her family's lives face a harrowing challenge as this terminal degenerative neurological ailment slowly progresses to an inevitable ending they all dread. Along the way, Alice struggles to not only fight the inner decay, but to make the most of her remaining time to find the love and peace to make simply living worthwhile.

Summary

While linguists may share a number of assumptions about language, they approach the study of language from different theoretical perspectives because linguists influenced by Noam Chomsky's views on language believe that language is primarily a product of the mind, and they are more concerned with studying linguistic competence—the unconscious knowledge of rules that every human possesses. Other linguists take a more expansive view of language, believing that it is just as valuable to study language in social contexts and to consider the structure of texts as well as the structure of sentences occurring in texts. In the following chapters, we will continue to study main areas of general linguistics.

Learning Highlights: Read and Think—Linguistics and Life

Linguistics is the scientific study of language, which reveals our life and society. Marx and Engels proposed that language and thought are not independent; instead, they are the reflection of actual life:

Language is the immediate actuality of thought. Just as philosophers have given thought an independent existence, so they were bound to make language into an independent realm. This is a secret of philosophical language, in which thoughts in the form of words have their own content. The problem of descending from the world of thoughts to the actual world is turned into the problem of descending from language to life.

Considering that connecting linguistics with life is a significant part in linguistics learning, we have arranged the section of "linguistics and life" for each chapter. In this chapter, let us think about linguistic system and life.

1. How do we study language?
2. How is linguistics learned?
3. How is language organised?

- **The Equality of Language**

It was created not by some one class, but by the entire society, by all the classes of the society, by the efforts of hundreds of generations.

Language is not a product of one or another base, old or new, within the given society, but of the whole course of the history of the society and of the history of the bases for many centuries. It was created not by some one class, but by the entire society, by all the classes of the society, by the efforts of hundreds of generations. It was created for the satisfaction of the needs not of one particular class, but of the entire society, of all the classes of the society. Precisely for this reason it was created as a single language for the society, common to all members of that society, as the common language of the whole people. Hence the functional role of language, as a means of intercourse between people, consists not in serving one class to the detriment of other classes, but in equally serving the entire society, all the classes of society. This in fact explains why a language may equally serve both the old, moribund system and the new, rising system; both the old base and the new base; both the exploiters and the exploited.

Marx and Engels proposed that language does not belong to any class, and that it should serve the entire society equally.

1. Do you agree that language has equality?
2. Can you give any example of the equality of language in real life?

● **Language Rises out of Our Curiosity about Life**

... Language is the most accessible part of the mind. People want to know about language because they hope this knowledge will lead to insight about human nature...

Inspired by Chomsky's Universal Grammar (UG), Brown has tried to characterize the Universal People (UP). He has scrutinized archives of ethnography for universal patterns underlying the behaviour of all documented human cultures, keeping a sceptical eye out both for claims of the exotic belied by the ethnographers' own reports, and for claims of the universal based on flimsy evidence. The outcome is stunning. Far from finding arbitrary variation, Brown was able to characterize the Universal People in gloriously rich detail. His findings contain something to startle almost anyone, and so I will reproduce the substance of them here. According to Brown, the Universal People have the following:

Value placed on articulateness. Gossip. Lying. Misleading. Verbal humour. Humorous insults. Poetic and rhetorical speech forms. Narrative and storytelling. Metaphor....

So we know human nature from learning language.
1. Can you find the universality of language?
2. Do you agree with the Universal People theory?

Let's consider some other characteristics of linguistics.

- **The Complexity of Linguistics**

Alice Munro said, "The complexity of things, things within things, just seems to be endless. I mean nothing is easy, nothing is simple." Learning linguistics is the same. Linguistics is the scientific study of language, and language is considered as the most complex of all human knowledge. Language is passively generated on the basis of "language competence", so it has complexity. Modern linguistics, on the other hand, is specifically about reducing its complexity and studying a branch of linguistic like syntax, semantics or pragmatics.

- **Linguistics Is a Systematic Study**

Linguistic theory expresses such invariants in the form of a model of a linguistic description, of which each empirically successful linguistic description is an instance, exemplifying every aspect of the model. In particular, linguistic descriptions describe the diverse ways in which different natural languages realize the abstract structure exhibited in the model; the model itself describes the form of a system of empirical generalizations capable of organizing and expressing the facts about a natural language.

- **The Hierarchical Linguistic Framework**

The modern linguistic framework has several subsystems, and within each subsystem there are hierarchical relationships. For example, applied linguistics contains branches such as psycholinguistics, sociolinguistics. Therefore, modern linguistics has a hierarchical nature, which is expressed in the fact that each level is a relationship between the containing and the contained.

Self-Study Activities

1. Match the structures in the left-hand column with the areas of linguistics in which they are studied in the right-hand column.

   (1) the structure of words　　　　　a. phonetics/phonology
   (2) word order/structure of clauses　　b. morphology
   (3) the meaning of words　　　　　　c. syntax

(4) individual sounds   d. semantics

2. If you are studying rules of syntax, are you studying linguistic competence or linguistic performance?

3. What is the difference between prescriptivist and descriptivist approaches to language study?

4. Do you agree that Chinese is syntactically different from English?

5. If you claim that the sentence "China home to the world's highest mountains" is "incorrect" are you making a judgment about the grammaticality of the sentence or its acceptability?

6. While a language such as French has a system of "grammatical" gender, English has "natural gender." What's the difference between the two systems, and, in particular, why is it the case that Modern English employs a system of "natural" gender?

Further Reading

A good introduction to Noam Chomsky's theory of generative grammar can be found in Steven Pinker's *The Language Instinct: How the Mind Creates Language* (New York: Harper Perennial Modern Classics, 2007).

For a critique of Chomsky's views on language, see Geoffrey Sampson's *The Language Instinct Debate* (London: Continuum International Publishing Group, 2005).

Functional grammar is described in detail in M. A. K. Halliday and C. M. I. M. Matthiessen's *An Introduction to Functional Grammar* (3rd ed.) (London: Hodder Arnold, 2004).

Outline

I. Linguistics, the scientific study of language, is informed by a long history of the study of grammar, and many of the ideas central to current linguistic theory go back to ancient times.

A. We define linguistics as a discipline that concerns itself with the study of all aspects of the present day but with a methodological outlook firmly based on the working practices developed in modern contemporary linguistics.

B. Linguistics is also found in other areas of study, including philosophy, anthropology, computer science, psychology, and speech pathology, and it is becoming more and more central to the study of language and literature in English departments and to the study of language acquisition, learning, and teaching in modern languages departments.

C. We can acquire the necessary tools to study languages in general (linguistics), the variety in language, the uses to which people put languages (sociolinguistics), the ways in which people teach and learn languages (applied linguistics) and the value of the study of language in understanding the human mind (psycholinguistics).

II. Language is a set of signals by which we communicate. Language is what makes us human, and we all seem to be naturally curious about it. Human language is not only a vocal system of communication. It can be expressed in writing, which is not limited in time or space. Besides, each language is both arbitrary and systematic.

A. Although speech and writing are in theory distinct, they can and do influence each other. Although speech and writing have much in common, they are not to be equated or hierarchically ordered; they are complementary, both necessary in a technologically advanced society.

B. Language is a two-way process involving both production and reception.

III. Language was defined above as a sign system which has two parts: lexicon and grammar. Language has three sorts of substructure: phonology, morphology, and syntax. Grammar is the linguistic rule system that we use to produce and understand sentences, which can be divided into four parts: phonetics, phonology, morphology, and semantics. Besides grammar, we are also concerned with the meaning of language in different contexts.

A. Phonetics is the study of human speech sounds. It studies what people do with their tongue, mouth, lips and lungs in order to produce speech sounds. It also studies the properties of how speech travels through the air—the sound waves.

B. Phonology is how speech sounds are used in any given language. It is the grammar of speech sounds. Not every language uses human language as speech sounds, or we can say there is no language using every possible human speech sound. Every language treats these sounds differently in

1 Introduction

interesting ways.

C. Morphology can be simply defined as the study of words, like how words are formed, how prefixes and suffixes are related to each other, and how a single word uses different prefixes and suffixes to have different meanings.

D. Syntax is the study of sentence structure, concerning how words are arranged in sentences to mean different things.

E. Semantics is the study of the meaning of words.

F. Pragmatics is the study of how humans use language in different contexts to understand speech. It is very important if you learn a foreign language and different cultures on your own.

2 Phonetics

2.1 Introduction

This chapter provides an overview of the sound system of English. It begins with a discussion of the smallest unit of sound, the phoneme, and continues with a description of the English alphabet and how it differs from the international phonetic alphabet (IPA). The phonetic symbols for English consonants and vowels are then presented and classified according to three criteria: *voicing* (whether the vocal cords vibrate or not), *place of articulation* (where in the mouth the sound is produced), and manner of articulation (how the airstream flows in the mouth during the articulation).

Phonetics differs from phonology in that it focuses on the mechanics of sound production and transmission, irrespective of how the sounds may operate as part of a language system; phonology focuses on the "function", or "organisation", or "patterning" of the sounds.

Phonetics is the systematic study of the sounds of speech, which is physical and directly observable. Phonetics is sometimes seen as not properly linguistic, because it is the outward, physical manifestation of the main object of linguistic research.

Phonetics, often described as the scientific study of speech production, is concerned with (a) the processes that generate an air-stream which carries *linguistic content* (**articulatory phonetics**), (b) the physical characteristics of the resulting sound waves that pass between the speaker's vocal tract and the listener's ears (**acoustic phonetics**), and (c) the processes whereby the mechanical movements of the ear-drum, created by the action of the sound waves, are transmitted into the middle and inner ear and perceived at a cortical level as sound (**auditory phonetics**). The term English phonetics refers to the description of the sounds encountered in English as a world-wide language.

Much of phonetic theory and description relates to articulatory phonetics; experimental phonetics (occasionally still called instrumental phonetics) refers to the study of phonetic data by means of instrumentation for the study of postures and movements of the speech organs (e.g. medical instrumentation, especially MRI) and the resulting acoustic patterns (e.g. software for acoustic analysis).

The discipline which underpins the description of the articulatory aspect of the sounds in all languages is *general phonetics*.

2.2 Speech Organs

Human beings are capable of producing an infinite number of sounds, but no language uses more than a small proportion of this infinite set and no two human languages make use of exactly the same set of sounds. When we speak, there is continuous movement of such organs as the tongue, the velum (soft palate), the lips and the lungs. We put spaces between individual words in the written medium but there are no similar spaces in speech. Words are linked together in speech and are normally perceived by one who does not know the language (or by a machine) as an uninterrupted stream of sound. We shall, metaphorically, slow the process down as we examine the organs of speech and the types of sound that result from using different organs.

The main organs of speech include the jaw, the lips, the teeth, the teeth ridge (usually called the alveolar ridge), the tongue, the hard palate, the soft palate (the velum), the uvula, the pharynx, the larynx and the vocal cords. The mobile organs are the lower jaw, the lips, the tongue, the velum, the uvula, the pharynx and the vocal cords. Although it is possible to learn to move each of these at will, we have the most control over the jaw, lips and tongue. The tongue is so important in the production of speech sounds that, for ease of reference, it has been divided into four main areas, the lips, the blade (or lamina), the front

and the back. (see Figure 2.1)

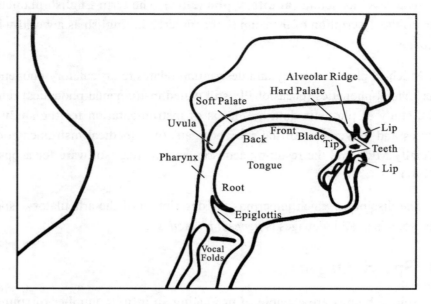

Figure 2.1   Speech organs.

2.3 Sounds of Language

The alphabet shows that there exist 26 sounds in English language. In fact, there are quite a few more. English has 44 different sounds. The alphabet only reflects the reality of English sounds approximately.

Sounds can be divided into two main types. As the central sound in the word "cat" is a vowel. The first and third sounds are consonants. More will be said about vowels and consonants in this chapter but these rough definitions will serve our purpose temporarily.

2.3.1 Consonants

There are many consonant sounds in English, but there are only twenty-four consonant phonemes of English—the sounds that make a difference in the meanings of words to English speakers. For example, in English the sounds /b/ and /p/ are distinctive, which means we hear the difference between them, and we know that the words *bit* and *pit* have different meanings. *Bit* and *pit* are a **minimal pair**, two words that differ by only a single phoneme in the same

2 Phonetics

position. The version of the IPA we use in this chapter is a representation of the phonemes of English, the sounds that we recognise as distinct from one another. When we write words using the IPA (International Phonetic Alphabet, see Figure 2.2), we are doing **phonemic transcription**. With phonemic transcription, there's always a one-to-one correspondence between sounds and symbols. It's important to remember that these symbols are not the same as letters and that they represent the sounds of language, not the letters of a writing system. We will describe each consonant in terms of each of the following:

- **Voicing:** Controlling the vibration of the vocal cords as air passes through to make speech sounds.
- **Place of articulation:** The places in the oral cavity where airflow is modified to make speech sounds.
- **Manner of articulation:** The way we move and position our lips, tongue and teeth to make speech sounds.

The ways in which we describe sounds within each of these categories—where and how the sound is made and whether there is vibration of the vocal cords—isolates a particular group of sounds, described as a natural class of sounds; sounds in a natural class share some set of phonetic characteristics, or phonetic features.

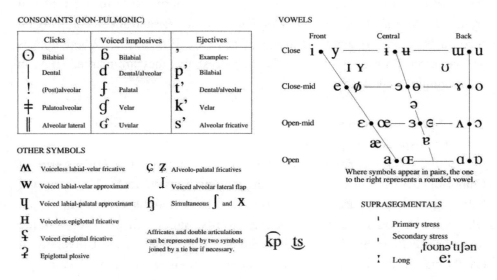

19

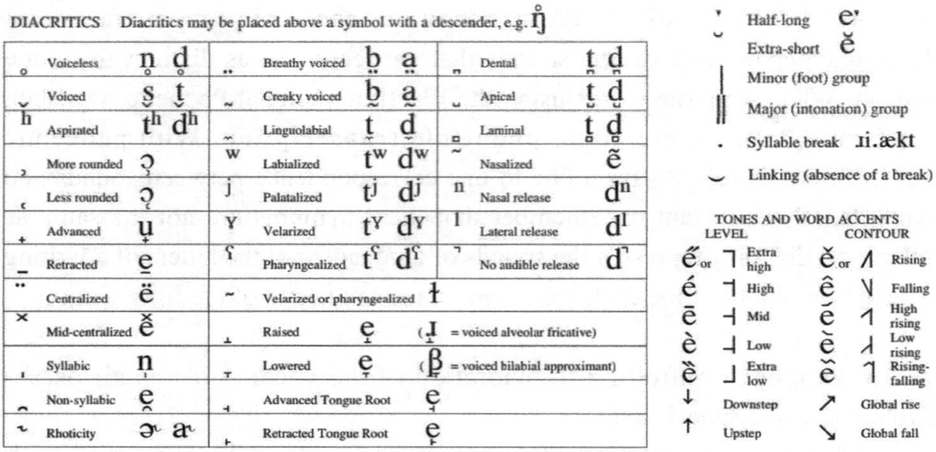

Figure 2.2 International phonetic alphabet.
(Source:www.arts.gla.ac.uk/ipa/fullchart; and International Phonetic Association 2005.)

Learning and Research Resources

• **The IPA Chart**

http://www.langsci.ucl.ac.uk/ipa/index.html.

The IPA chart is reprinted with the permission of the International Phonetic Association. We are grateful to the IPA for the permission to use material from the *Journal of the IPA*, the *Handbook of the IPA* and the accompanying recordings, which are available to members via the IPA website. Where images are based on IPA recordings from the website above, they are marked (IPA) in the accompanying captions.

• **Speak and Improve**

https://speakandimprove.com/

Speak and Improve is a research project from the University of Cambridge. By free using it you are helping us improve technology that will help English learners around the world. You can talk to a speech robot, Sandi, who will ask you some questions. Afterwards, Sandi will give you a grade for your speaking. Sandi uses new technology developed at the University of Cambridge. It can tell how well you speak English just by listening to you.

> ● *L'enfant sauvage/ The Wild Child* (Film)
> *The Wild Child* (French: *L'Enfant sauvage*) is a 1970 French film, and it tells the story of a child who spends the first eleven or twelve years of his life with little or no human contact. One summer day in 1798, a naked boy of 11 or 12 years of age is found in a forest in the rural district of Aveyron in southern France. Living like a wild animal and unable to speak or understand language, the child has apparently grown up in solitude in the forest since an early age. Afterwards, under the patient tutelage of the doctor and his housekeeper, Victor gradually becomes socialized and acquires the rudiments of language.

Many of the symbols in the IPA are based on the Roman alphabet: this does not mean necessarily that their sound values will be those of such letters in the Roman alphabet itself. Thus, the [c] symbol, for a voiceless palatal plosive, is not used in a phonemic transcription of English. The word *cat* would be written in IPA not with a [c] as its first sound, but with a [k] (The symbol [c] is, however, sometimes needed when transcribing the speech of young children or certain speech pathologies or some adult pronunciations of /k/ and /g/ before front close vowels, e.g. in keen, geese.). In phonemic notations, it is usual practice to choose as the representative of the phoneme the most appropriate symbol. For the /r/ phoneme in English, despite [r], a voiced alveolar trill that is a relatively infrequent realization of the phoneme, the choice of the phoneme symbol is dictated by the ease with which the [r] symbol is associated with the particular phoneme by dint of the orthographic conventions of <r> in English. Angle brackets < > enclose normal orthographic forms in the Roman alphabet.

Group-Work Activities

> ● Pinyin vs IPA
> "言语异声，文字异性。"——《史记·秦始皇本纪》

"The Pinyin system uses Roman alphabets to spell the sounds of Chinese characters, but it was not designed as an accurate phonetic transcription system. ...Mandarin is written in Chinese characters, but characters do not provide consistent information about pronunciations. In general, pronunciation cannot be derived from looking at Chinese characters, although sometimes characters with common parts have similar pronunciation. Unlike most languages, <u>Chinese characters are not primarily phonetic, and certainly not alphabetic, but pictographic or ideographic</u> (displaying combinations of pictures or symbols to convey meaning) like ancient Egyptian hieroglyphics. Hence there has needed to be a way of representing in writing the pronunciation of each character when teaching the language. Therefore, Putonghua is typically studied via a transcription. Many transcription systems have been devised for Mandarin Chinese in China and in the West. Most of these are based on the Roman alphabet, and are therefore termed 'romanization' systems." (Odinye, *Phonology of Mandarin Chinese: A comparison of Pinyin and IPA*.)

1. Can you figure out any advantages or disadvantages of using IPA and Pinyin?
2. How do you understand the underlined sentence?
3. Do you agree that "Putonghua is typically studied via a transcription?" Please explain your answer.
4. What do you think about the influence of "romanization systems" on Putonghua?
5. Please find some studies about Pinyin and the IPA and compare the differences of the two systems.

2.3.2 Voiced and Voiceless Consonants

All consonants are either *voiced* or *voiceless*. The airflow coming out of the lungs can meet resistance at the *larynx*, or voice box. The resistance can be controlled by the different positions of and tensions in the vocal cords or vocal folds, which are two muscular bands of tissue that stretch from front to back in the larynx, behind the Adam's apple. When you're breathing, the vocal folds are relaxed and spread apart to allow air to flow freely from the lungs. When you have the right amount of air and tension of the muscles in the cords, they vibrate when you speak. This is called voicing. You can feel this vocal fold vibration when you are producing a sound. Put your hand on your throat and make the sound [s] Keep your hand there and switch to [z]. (We are using brackets here to simply refer to a sound without reference to whether or not it is a phoneme.). You can feel the vibration of your vocal cords—that's **voicing**. It happens with other sound pairs too, but it can be harder to feel because the sounds are shorter. For example, [p] and [b] differ only in vocal cord vibration, but because the sounds are so short, it's harder to feel them. (Beware: When we produce these sounds, we tend to add a vowel to them, making it more like "puh" or "buh."

Table 2.1 Consonant Phonemes of English

place \ manner	Bilabial		Labiodental		Interdental		Alveolar		Palatal		Velar		Glottal	
Stop	p	p					t	d			k	g		
Fricative			f	v	θ	ð	s	z	š	ž				
Affricative									č	ǰ				
Nasal		m						n				ŋ		
Glide	m	w								y				h
Liquid								l r						

☐ = voiceless   ☐ =voiced

Note: You may prefer to use the following alternative symbols for the palatal affricates and fricatives: š = ʃ, ž = ʒ, č = tʃ, and ǰ = dʒ.

2.3.3 Places of Articulation

The various parts of the mouth and throat used to make speech sounds are called the articulators.

All consonant sounds involve some degree of obstruction or obstructions to the air-stream. The obstruction is specified by manner of articulation (the type of obstruction) and the place of articulation (the location of the obstruction within the vocal tract.

Bilabial

The bilabial (from the Latin *bi*-"two" and *labial* "lips") sounds are made with both lips. The sounds in this group are all made by bringing both lips together or almost together.

Labiodental

The two sounds in the labiodental (from the Latin *labio* "lip" and *dent* "tooth") group are made with the lower lip against the upper front teeth.

Table 2.2 Place of Articulation of English Consonants

Bilabial	lips	[p] [pʰ] [b] [m]	pan, ban, man
Labio-dental	lower lip and upper teeth	[f] [v]	fish, living, red (for some speakers)
Dental	tongue and upper teeth	[θ] [ð]	thigh, thy
Alveolar	tip and rims of the tongue and upper alveolar ridge and side teeth	[tʰ] [t] [d] [s] [z] [n] [l]	ten, den, Len, send, Zen, net, (for some speakers) red
Post-alveolar	tip, blade, and rims of the tongue and rear part of upper alveolar ridge	[r]	red
Palato-alveolar	tip, blade, and rims of the tongue and upper alveolar ridge and side teeth	[ʃ] [ʒ] [tʃ] [dʒ]	chain, Jane
Velar	tongue and soft palate	[kʰ] [k] [g] [ŋ]	cat, get, sing
Glottal	vocal cords	[ʔ] [h]	help

Interdental

The two sounds in the interdental (from the Latin *inter* "between" and *dent* "tooth") group are made with the tip of the tongue between the front teeth.

It can be difficult at first to distinguish between these two sounds because we aren't used to doing so (since they are both written with <th>). The name of the /θ/ symbol is *theta*, which begins with the voiceless /ð/ sound, and the name for the /ð/ symbol is *eth*, which contains the voiced /ð/ sound.

Alveolar

The sounds in this group are made with the tongue tip at or near the *alveolar ridge*. To find your alveolar ridge, put your tongue on the back of your top teeth and slide it upward. That bump, or ridge, is the alveolar ridge. (It might not be obvious to you that /r/ is an alveolar sound because your tongue seems to be rather scrunched up.

Palatal

The sounds in this group are made with the tongue near your *palate*, the hard part of the roof of the mouth. Slide your tongue back from your alveolar ridge to find your palate.

The alternative symbols /ʃ/, /ʒ/, /tʃ/, and /dʒ/ may be substituted for /š/, /ž/, /č /, and /ǰ/, respectively.

Velar

The sounds in this group are made with the tongue near the *velum*, the soft part of the roof of your mouth, behind the palate.

Glottal

This is a sound made at the *glottis*, the space between the vocal folds.

The sound /h/ is sometimes classified as a glottal fricative. There is another sound of English, though it is not typically counted as a distinct phoneme, represented by the symbol /ʔ/. It is the sound in the middle of the word uh-oh, where there is a stoppage of airflow at the glottis; it is, therefore, classified as a glottal stop.

2.3.4 Manner of Articulation

Each consonant sound is also described by means of its manner of articulation, that is, how the sound is made, especially with respect to airflow.

Table 2.3 Manner of Articulation of English Consonants

Plosive / stop	articulatory organs form obstruction; Air stream is held up; sudden release of air	[pʰ] [p] [tʰ] [t] [kʰ] [k] [ʔ] [b] [d] [g]	pink, ball, teeth, dog, kiss, gear
Fricative	articulatory organs brought so close together that friction of air stream occurs	[f] [v] [θ] [ð] [s] [z] [ʃ] [ʒ] [h]	fast, valley, thick, though, sea, zenith, shell, genre, measure
Affricate	plosive with friction during release stage	[tʃ] [dʒ]	cheers, jam
Lateral	partial closure so that air stream can escape on one or both sides of obstruction	[l]	let, lonely, all
Approximant	contraction of tongue; air stream can escape without friction	[r] [w] [j]	wear, yellow, yawn
Nasal	air stream released through nose; articulatory organs form obstruction	[n] [m] [ŋ]	make, nut, bun, sing

Stops
The sounds in this group are made by obstructing the airstream completely in the oral cavity. All the symbols shown here have the same pronunciation as they do in the example words given with the places of articulation.

Fricatives
The sounds in this group are made by forming a nearly complete stoppage of the airstream.

Affricates
The sounds in this group are made by briefly stopping the airstream completely and then releasing the articulators slightly so that friction is produced; these sounds start as stops and finish as fricatives.

An affricate is a plosive followed immediately by a fricative at the same place of articulation. In the words chess and Jack, the initial consonants are postalveolar plosives and postalveolar fricatives. Note that the IPA symbolization [T] and [D] obscures the fact that both plosive elements are postalveolar, not alveolar; for this reason, some phoneticians use non-IPA [c] and [j] for these sounds.

Nasals
The sounds in this group are made by lowering the velum and letting the airstream pass primarily through the nasal cavity.

Glides
The sounds in this group are made with only a slight closure of the articulators—if the vocal tract were any more open, the result would be a vowel.

Liquids
The sounds in this group are produced when an obstruction is formed by the articulators but is not narrow enough to stop the airflow or to cause friction. The /l/ is often described as a *lateral* liquid, because for most speakers the tongue touches the roof of the mouth near the alveolar ridge, and air flows around the sides of the tongue. As mentioned above, the /r/ is described as a

bunched liquid because for most American English speakers the tongue is just bunched up under the palate during the production of the sound.

2.4 Vowels

By definition, a vowel sound, unlike a consonant sound, should offer no obstruction to the air-stream. As far back as the mid-nineteenth century, phoneticians held the view that two parameters govern the production of a vowel sound: the configuration of the tongue surface and the position and shaping of the lips. Due to the tongue's mobility and the fact that in almost all vowel sounds the tongue's upper surface assumes a convex shape, it has normally been found sufficient to plot the position of the highest part of the tongue along two axes: the horizontal and the vertical. The possible trajectories of the tongue in the production of vowel sounds then lead to the establishment of the so "called vowel" space beneath the hard and soft palates, whose outer limits are represented in the cardinal vowel diagram. The latter provides not only a schema of the vowel-space, but also a set of auditory and articulatory *reference* points along those outer limits, similar to the principle of the cardinal points of a compass. There are 18 Cardinal Vowels, set up in the early 1900s by the English phonetician Daniel Jones. However, normally four additional vowels, as well as a set of non-Cardinal vowels, are added to the set.

2.4.1 Monophthongs

Vowels are determined by three paraments: *height, frontness* and *roundedness*. Vowels between the front and back vowels are called the central vowels. The last two English vowels occur in the central region.

Most languages have three to seven vowels. English, however, has fourteen to twenty vowels, depending on the dialects. Table 2.4 includes the vowels of most dialects of American English (though not the diphthongs—we'll get to those soon). The position labels (high, back, etc.) are descriptions that refer to the position of the tongue in the mouth. Though it may be slightly more difficult to determine where your tongue is with vowels than with consonants, your tongue does move. Say the words *beet, bet, bat*, and feel how your tongue lowers with each word.

In English alphabet, there are five vowels: *a, e, i, o,* and *u*. In school, we learn that there are actually "long" and "short" versions of vowels, e.g. "short *a*" in *cat* and "long *a*" in *father*. The reality of English vowels is, in fact, even richer, as we can see from how vowels are rendered in the IPA. Like consonants, vowels are produced in the mouth in ways that have nothing to do with the order *a, e, i, o, u*.

Table 2.4　Monophthongal Vowel Phonemes of English

	Front	Central	Back
High	i ɪ		u ʊ
Mid	e ɛ	ə ʌ	o ɔ
Low	æ		a

2.4.2　Diphthongs

In addition to the vowels shown in Table 2.4, English has phonemic diphthongs, two-part vowel sounds consisting of a vowel and a glide in one syllable. In English, they are /ai/ (rice), /aʊ/ (house), and /ɔi/ (boil). In many dialects, if you say eye slowly, you can feel the two parts of the vowel sound. Diphthongs are distinguished from two single vowels.

Vowels differ between GA (General American) and RP (Received Pronunciation). Because RP is non-rhotic, it has many more diphthongs than GA. GA and RP share three diphthongs:

/ai/ fight　　　　　/aʊ/ house　　　　　/ɔi/ boy

In each of the diphthongs above, the tongue changes position as each part of the diphthong is articulated. In the case of /ɔi/, for instance, the tongue is initially positioned in the lower back part of the mouth and then "glides" to the upper front of the mouth. This feature of diphthongs explains why in the American tradition of transcription, the three diphthongs above are transcribed, respectively, as /ay/, /aw/ and /ɔy/. The sounds /y/ and /w/, sometimes referred to as glides (or semi-vowels), are used to reflect the gradual transition between vowels inherent in diphthongs.

While GA and RP share three diphthongs, RP has four additional diphthongs occurring in syllables where GA would have a vowel /ɹ/ sequence, a sequence leading to an /ɹ/-coloured vowel.

Thus, the four words below would have different pronunciations in GA and RP:

	GA	RP
fear	/fiɹ/	/fiə/
fair	/fɛɹ/	/feə/
tire	/taiɹ/	/taə/
four	/foʊɹ/	/fʊə/

In GA, any time a vowel occurs before an /ɹ/ in a single syllable, the /ɹ/ colours the vowel, creating a single sound in a sense. In RP, in contrast, no such sequences of vowel /ɹ/ exist, resulting instead in a diphthong.

2.4.3 Great Vowel Shift

During the Middle English period, the seven tense vowels of the predominant dialect in the language underwent a shift known now as the *Great Vowel Shift*. It was a gradual process that began in Chaucer's time (the fourteenth century) and continued through the time of Shakespeare (the early seventeenth century). Table 2.5 illustrates the shift: One vowel's articulation point was raised, and this shifted the next vowel up; however, the highest vowels had no higher place to go, so those two vowels, /u:/ and /i:/, became diphthongs. So the early English speakers lived in a /hu:s/, milked a /ku:/ for /swe:t/ milk. Some English speakers, primarily in Scotland, still maintain the pre-Great Vowel Shift pronunciation. The table illustrates all of the shifts and sample words' pre-shift and post-shift pronunciations. One of the primary reasons that this vowel shift has become known as the "Great' Vowel Shift" is that it profoundly affected English phonology, and these changes coincided with the introduction of the printing press. William Caxton brought the first mechanized printing press to England in 1476. Prior to mechanized printing, words in the handwritten texts had been spelled pretty much, however, each particular scribe wanted to spell them according to the scribe's own dialect. Even after the printing press, however, most printers used the spellings that had begun to be established, not realizing the significance of the vowel changes that were under way. By the time the vowel shifts were complete in the early 1600s, hundreds of books had been printed which used a spelling system reflecting the pre-Great Vowel Shift pronunciation. So, the word goose, for example, had two "o" s to indicate a long /o/ sound, /o:/—a good, phonetic spelling of the word. However, the vowel had shifted to /u/; thus *goose, moose, food* and other similar words that we now spell with "oo" have mismatched spelling and pronunciation.

Table 2.5 The Great Vowel Shift

		Front	Central	Back	
High	[fi:f]→ [fayf] "five"	i:		u:	[hu:s]→ [haws] "house"
Mid	[swe:t]→[swit] "sweet"	e:		o:	[fo:d]→ [fu:d] "food"
	[dɛ:g] → [de] "day"	ɛ:		ɔ:	[stɔ:n] → [ston] "stone"
Low			ay aw	a:	[na:mə] → [nem] "name"

Why didn't printers just change the spelling to match the pronunciation? Because by this time, the increased volume of book production, combined with increasing literacy, resulted in a powerful force against spelling change. Other vowel shifts are going on all the time, in all dialects of English, all over the world.

How a linguist transcribes a word and how we are used to seeing it spelled can differ considerably. For example, many people are using the "proper" rule, because words that we think of as beginning with a vowel are often pronounced with an initial glottal stop—a consonant.

2.5 Sounds beyond Those in English

Each language fills in only part of this "grid." Other languages have consonants that fill in places in this grid that are empty in English. For example, the *ch* sound in *Bach* is a velar fricative, indicated with [x].

Japanese people pronounce Fuji in a fashion that sounds, to us, as if they simply "have an accent." However, their sound is not an [f] at all but a bilabial fricative, indicated with [ɸ].

The throaty *r* we learn in French classes is, in terms of place of articulation, *uvular*—it is a voiced uvular fricative, indicated with capital *r* written upside down [ʁ].

Group-Work Activities

● **Phonemic Awareness and Classical Chinese Poetry**
1. Do you know what is the phonemic awareness?
Phonemic awareness is the ability to identify and manipulate individual sounds (phonemes) in spoken words. It is the understanding that spoken language words can be broken into individual phonemes—the smallest unit of spoken language. Phonemic awareness is not the same as phonics—phonemic awareness focuses on the individual sounds in spoken language. As students begin to move to phonics, they learn the relationship between a phoneme (sound) and grapheme (the letter(s) that represent the sound) in written language.

赠别	Old Love
杜牧	Du Mu
多情却似总无情，	Old love would seem as though not love today,
唯觉樽前笑不成。	Spell-bound by thee, my laughter dies away.
蜡烛有心还惜别，	The very wax sheds sympathetic tears,
替人垂泪到天明。	And gutters sadly down till dawn appears.

送元二使安西	Seeing Off Yuan Second on a Mission to An[x]i
王维	Wang Wei
渭城朝雨浥轻尘，	The light dust in the town of Wei is wet with morning rain,
客舍青青柳色新。	Green, green, the willows by the guest house their yearly freshness regain.
劝君更尽一杯酒，	Be sure to finish yet another cup of wine, my friend,
西出阳关无故人。	West of the Yang Gate no old acquaintance will you meet again!

| 赠孟浩然 | To Meng Haoran |
| 李白 | Li Bai |

吾爱孟夫子，	O Master Meng my friend! How I love thee,
风流天下闻。	Whose spirited ways to all the world known!
红颜弃轩冕，	White-head'd thou seek'st to lie beneath pine tree,
白首卧松云。	As in fair youth thou spurned Rank and Gown.
醉月频中圣，	Beneath the moon too oft thy cup thou'dst fill,
迷花不事君。	And be rather charmed by flowers than the King to serve.
高山安可仰，	Thy Virtue fragrant, like a lofty hill,
徒此揖清芬。	I can but homage pay that thou deserve.

2. Do you think these poems (both Chinese and English version) have rhyme scheme?

3. Do you think Chinese poetry is intrinsically better suited to rhyming than English versification?

4. Which sounds make the rhyme scheme in each poem and its English version?

Learning and Research Resources

- **Top 5 Phonetic Journals**

There are numerous journals where phoneticians can publish their papers. It might be interesting to look closer into the current situation and identify important periodicals accepting primarily papers covering topics in phonetics and phonology, or those that are of professional interest to phoneticians for one reason or another.

1. *Journal of the International Phonetic Association*

https://www.cambridge.org/core/journals/journal-of-the-international-phonetic-association.

This journal is a forum for work in the fields of phonetic theory and description. As well as including papers on laboratory phonetics/phonology and related topics, the journal encourages submissions on practical applications of phonetics to areas such as phonetics teaching and speech therapy, as well as the analysis of speech phenomena in relation to computer speech processing. It is especially concerned with the theory behind the International Phonetic Alphabet and discussions of the use of symbols for illustrating the phonetic structures of a wide variety of languages.

2. *The Journal of Phonetics*

https://www.sciencedirect.com/journal/journal-of-phonetics.

The Journal of Phonetics publishes papers of an experimental or theoretical nature that deal with phonetic aspects of language and linguistic communication processes. Papers dealing with technological and/or pathological topics, or papers of an interdisciplinary nature are also suitable, provided that linguistic-phonetic principles underlie the work reported.

3. *Phonetica*

https://www.karger.com/Journal/Home/224275.

Phonetica is an international interdisciplinary forum for phonetic science that covers all aspects of the subject matter, from phonetic and phonological descriptions of segments and prosodies to speech physiology, articulation, acoustics, perception, acquisition, and phonetic variation and change. It provides a platform for a comprehensive understanding of speaker-hearer interaction across languages and dialects, and of learning contexts throughout the lifespan.

4. *Phonology*

https://www.cambridge.org/core/journals/phonology

Phonology is the only journal devoted to all aspects of the discipline, and provides a unique forum for the productive interchange of ideas among phonologists and those working in related disciplines. Preference is given to papers which make a substantial theoretical contribution, irrespective of the particular theoretical framework employed, but the submission of papers presenting new empirical data of general theoretical interest is also encouraged.

5. *The Journal of the Acoustical Society of America*

https://asa.scitation.org/journal/jas

It is a journal in the field of acoustics, published by the Acoustical Society of America. It contains technical articles on sound, vibration, speech and other topics. The journal has been the leading source of theoretical and experimental research results in the broad interdisciplinary subject of sound.

Summary

The study of sounds can focus on either individual segments (phonemes) or suprasegmentals (we will examine them in the next chapter). Like all languages, English has a distinctive set of speech segments called phonemes: consonants and vowels that make up the inventory of sounds in English. It is possible to determine which sounds in English are distinctive by examining minimal pairs: words that differ by a single phoneme. All English phonemes can be described in terms of their place of articulation where the tongue and lips are positioned when a sound is articulated and manner of articulation where the air flows in the oral or nasal cavities and the degree to which the airstream is obstructed or allowed to flow freely. Phonemes can also be voiced or unvoiced, depending upon whether the vocal cords vibrate or not.

Learning Highlights: Read and Think—Linguistics and Life

Learning phonetics raises our awareness of sounds in the real life.

1. Except human speech, can you find other sounds in life?
2. What are the characteristics of human speech?
3. Why are phoneticians so concerned with human speech?

Here are some features of human language that remain on almost every researcher's list:

- **Semanticity**

Specific signals can be matched with specific meanings. In short, words have meanings.

- **Arbitrariness**

There is no logical connection between the form of the signal and the thing it refers to. For example, dog in English is "hund" in German and "perro" in Spanish.

- **Discreteness**

Messages in the system are made up of smaller, repeatable parts rather than indivisible units. A word, for example, can be broken down into units of sound.

- **Displacement**

The language user can talk about things that are not present—the messages can refer to things in remote time (past and future) or space (here or elsewhere).

- **Productivity**

Language users can understand and create never-before-heard utterances.

- **Duality of Patterning**

A large number of meaningful utterances can be recombined in a systematic way from a small number of discrete parts of language. For example, suffixes can be attached to many roots, and words can be combined to create novel sentences.

Many animals have complex communicative interactions that do not share these features of human language. Consider, for example, the communication system of the African vervet monkey, as studied by Struhsaker (1967). In this system, there are three types of predators (leopard, eagle and snake), and there is a distinct call for each. A loud bark signals a leopard; a coughing sound signals an eagle; a chutter sound signals a snake. The vervet's packmates respond appropriately to the calls (running up a tree to safety from a leopard, diving into brush to hide from an eagle, or scanning the ground for a snake) even if they cannot see the predator.

1. Do you think animals have their "languages"?
2. Do you think sounds produced by animals can be termed as "language"?
3. Can you summarize the features of phonetics?

We can find the individuality in studying phonetics. For example, different people may have different voices. "As well as conveying a message in words and sounds, the speech signal carries information about the speaker's own anatomy, physiology, linguistic experience and mental state. These speaker characteristics are found in speech at all levels of description, from the spectral information in the sounds to the choice of words and utterances themselves."

1. Why can we find the individuality in studying phonetics?
2. Do you think there are the same voices in the world?

Self-Study Activities

1. What are the differences between vowels and consonants?

2. Please describe the following sounds in terms of voicing, place of articulation and manner of articulation.

Example: /p/ is a voiceless bilabial stop.

/f/ /ŋ/ /h/ /b/ /g/ /š/ /θ/ /č/ /n/ /t/ /r/ /m/

3. If we used a phonetic alphabet instead of the English alphabet for spelling, would it make English spelling easier?

4. Why do the words "fast" and "feast" justify that the sounds /æ/ and /i/ are phonemes in English?

5. For the table below, you are required to state the place of articulation, to explain the manner of articulation of each sound, and give an example of an English word beginning with the sound illustrated.

Place of articulation	Manner of articulation	Example

6. English has numerous allophones. For instance, the syllable-initial unvoiced plosives /p/, /t/, and /k/ are aspirated, but not in the medial or final position. Vowels are longer before voiced consonants than unvoiced consonants. In the list of words below, indicate which stops are aspirated, and which vowels are lengthened. Some words may not illustrate either of these processes; other words may illustrate both processes.

(1) pad   (2) tram   (3) grip   (4) sting   (5) stink   (6) play   (7) crab

7. Please find out words including the sound /l/.

(1) All the Chinese people, black-eyed and yellow-skinned, welcome you with open arms.

(2) Over the last 2,000 years, his philosophy has continued to influence China and the rest of the world.

(3) Scripts and painting spread widely in the world with the help of Yin Shua.

2 Phonetics

Further Reading

General introductions to phonetics can be found in Michael Ashby and John Maidment's *Introducing Phonetic Science* (Cambridge: Cambridge University Press, 2005) as well as Peter. Ladefoged's, *A Course in Phonetics* (4th ed., New York: Wadsworth Publishers, 2005).

Heinz J. Giegerich's *English Phonology* (Cambridge: Cambridge University Press, 1992) provides an overview of the systematic nature of the English sound system, with discussions of allophones and word stress.

Robert Stockwell and Donna Minkova's *English Words: History and Structure* (Cambridge: Cambridge University Press, 2001) describes word stress in a series of succinct rules (pp. 168–176).

Outline

I. Phonetics, often described as the scientific study of speech production, is concerned with
   A. articulatory phonetics, the processes that generate an airstream which carries linguistic content;
   B. acoustic phonetics, the physical characteristics of the resulting sound waves that pass between the speaker's vocal tract and the listener's ears;
   C. auditory phonetics, the processes whereby the mechanical movements of the ear-drum, created by the action of the sound waves, are transmitted into the middle and inner ear and perceived at a cortical level as sound.
II. The organs of speech include the jaw, the lips, the teeth, the teeth ridge (usually called the alveolar ridge), the tongue, the hard palate, the soft palate (the velum), the uvula, the pharynx, the larynx and the vocal cords.
III. Sounds can be divided into two main types.
   A. A vowel is a sound that needs an open-air passage in the mouth. The air passage can be modified in terms of shape with different mouth and tongue shapes producing different vowels.
   B. A consonant is formed when the air stream is restricted or stopped at some point between the vocal cords and the lips. The central sound in the word "cat" is a vowel.

Ⅳ. We will describe each consonant in terms of each of the following:

A. Voicing, controlling the vibration of the vocal cords as air passes through to make speech sounds;

B. Place of articulation, the places in the oral cavity where airflow is modified to make speech sounds.
  ⅰ) bilabial: [p] [b] [m]
  ⅱ) labio-dental: [f] [v]
  ⅲ) dental: [θ] [ð]
  ⅳ) alveolar: [t] [d] [s] [z] [n] [l]
  ⅴ) post-alveolar: [r]
  ⅵ) palate-alveolar: [ʃ] [ʒ] [tʃ] [dʒ]
  ⅶ) velar: [k] [g] [ŋ]
  ⅷ) glottal: [ʔ] [h]

C. Manner of articulation, the way we move and position our lips, tongue, and teeth to make speech sounds
  ⅰ) plosive/stop: [ph] [p] [th] [t] [kh] [k] [ʔ] [b] [d] [g]
  ⅱ) fricative: [f] [v] [θ] [ð] [s] [z] [ʃ] [ʒ] [h]
  ⅲ) affricative: [tʃ] [dʒ]
  ⅳ) lateral: [l]
  ⅴ) approximant: [r] [w] [j]
  ⅵ) nasal: [n] [m] [ŋ]

Ⅴ. Vowels are determined by three paraments: height, frontness, and roundedness. Vowels between the front and back vowels are called the central vowels.

Research Fronts

Zhang, Zheng, Yan and Jin (2019) did a research on father tongue hypothesis who proposed that the phonemic characteristics are related to father's tongue while the lexical characteristics are affected by mother's tongue. Here are some contents extracted from their article "Reconciling the father tongue and mother tongue hypotheses in Indo-European populations."

Mother Togue Hypothesis vs Father Togue Hypothesis

"The hypothesis that language usage follows matrilineal inheritance has been supported by genetic evidence, as in the Austronesian-speaking

populations and South American Indian. This is called as the mother tongue hypothesis sensu stricto. In contrast, on the basis of other findings from genetic and anthropological research, population geneticists and anthropologists advocate the father tongue hypothesis, which cites that a strong correlation exists between languages and Y-chromosomes."

Father Language and Lexical Characteristics vs Mother Language and Phonemic Characteristics

...the evolution of phonemic systems is more complicate. Phonemes can change not only diachronically but also synchronically, such as via contac tinduced (i.e. phoneme borrowings) or spontaneous evolution (i.e. Great Vowel Shift)....Some researchers suggest that in contrast to lexical systems, phonemic systems could be more conservative and provide earlier insights into the evolution of languages.

We showed that genetic and linguistic distances are significantly correlated with each other and that both are correlated with geographical distances among these populations. However, when controlling for geographical factors, only the correlation between the distances of paternal and lexical characteristics, and between those of maternal and phonemic characteristics, remained.

3 Phonology

3.1 Introduction

Phonology is the study of the sound system and the processes we use to discover the unconscious systems underlying our speech. Phonology involves two studies: the study of production, transmission and reception of speech sounds, a discipline known as "phonetics", and the study of the sounds and sound patterns of a specific language, a discipline known as "phonemics".

In the last chapter, we have learned about the sounds of English in isolation. In reality, however, linguistic sounds are not generally used in isolation; we string sounds together to make comprehensible words and sentences. When sounds are used together, they affect and influence each other in predictable and systematic ways.

3.2 Speech Segments

Speech segments can be either phonemes or allophones. In the last chapter, we mentioned that phonemes are distinctive speech sounds; that is, they create meaningful differences in words. One way to determine whether a speech sound is distinctive is to examine minimal pairs: words that differ by only a single phoneme in the same position in a word. For instance, the words *bat* and *cat* differ by only one sound: the second and third segments are the same vowel and consonant—/æ/ and /t/, respectively—but the two initial sounds are different. *Bat* begins with /b/ and *cat* with /k/. That *bat* and *cat* are different words provides evidence that the sounds /b/ and /k/ in English are phonemes. Indeed, considering other minimal pairs with these sounds points to their status as phonemes:

tack/tab   cake/bake   kind/bind

Phonemes are abstract representations of speech segments. Consequently, the words *pot* and *spot* both contain the phoneme /p/. However, if the actual pronunciation of these words is considered, it turns out that the phoneme /p/ is pronounced differently in the two words. When /p/ occurs at the start of a syllable, as in pot, it is **aspirated**: a puff of air accompanies the pronunciation of this sound. In contrast, when /p/ occurs in the middle of a syllable, as in spot, or at the end of a syllable, as in top, it is unaspirated. It is possible to actually feel the presence or absence of air by placing your hand in front of your mouth while pronouncing each of these three words. While aspirated and unaspirated /p/ are different sounds, they are not phonemes (at least in English) because they are not distinctive. It is not possible to create minimal pairs with these two sounds: there is no way to create two separate words in English that differ only by aspirated and unaspirated /p/. These two sounds are therefore considered allophones: predictable variations in pronunciation of a phoneme. The phoneme /p/ is aspirated initially in a syllable and unaspirated elsewhere. A later section will consider in greater detail other types of allophonic variation in English.

Languages vary in terms of the inventory of phonemes that they contain. While aspirated and unaspirated /p/ are not distinctive in English, in Hindi they are. English has the phoneme /ð/ at the beginning of a word such as *those*. German, a language that is very closely related to English, lacks this phoneme, using /d/ to begin words for the definite article, such as *die*, *der* and *das*. English distinguishes /ɹ/ and /l/ in words such as *right* and *light*, while many Asian languages, such as Japanese, do not.

Learning and Research Resources

● 国家哲学社会科学文献中心
http://www.ncpssd.org/index.aspx
National Centre for Philosophy and Social Science Documentation is an academic platform developed by the Central Committee of the Communist Party of China, led by the Chinese Academy of Social Sciences and constructed in

cooperation with the Ministry of Education of the People's Republic of China. This documentation centre provides a wealth of literature and information resources for philosophical and social scientists, and provides important assistance in promoting the innovative development of philosophy and social sciences.

Can you try to search any documentation about "Phoneme" in NCPSCD?

- 术语在线

https://www.termonline.cn/index

术语在线 (termonline.cn) is established as a terminology knowledge service platform, sponsored by the National Committee. It aims to promote scientific and technological exchanges and support scientific and technological development.

3.3 Allophones

The consonant chart has only one /p/. That's because there is only one /p/ phoneme in English. However, we'll see that it's useful to indicate that there are two allophones of /p/—two predictable pronunciations of the phoneme /p/—and it is completely predictable when we get one and when we get the other. Let's see how this works. Consider the data in the following two columns, and determine whether you have the aspiration or not on each of the /p/.

A	B
pat	spell
pickle	special
Peter	spare

In linguistic terms, "real sounds" are *phonemes*. The other sounds are *allophones* of a phoneme. In English, [b] and [p] are phonemes; [p^h] is merely an allophone of [p].

Allophones, although often represented by one letter of the alphabet, are quite central to how we express sounds. For example, because there are many allophones of the phoneme /l/, the word *oil* actually sounds virtually identical when played backward.

The words in column A all have an aspirated [p]. Those in column B have an unaspirated [p]. Here's one way to illustrate this fact:

3 Phonology

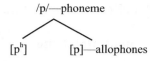

The superscript *h* in [pʰ] indicates the aspiration. This aspiration of the [p] occurs automatically in English when the /p/ is in a certain position with respect to other sounds and is what we will call a *phonological rule* of English. The following is one way to formally write the rule (the generalization) for the preceding data with the /p/s: /p/ becomes aspirated when it occurs at the beginning of a stressed syllable. Otherwise, it is unaspirated.

The aspiration rule of English applies not only to /p/ but to the natural class of voiceless stops in English, /p/, /t/, and /k/. So, the /t/ of *tack* is aspirated, but the /t/ of *stack* is not. The /k/ of *cat* is aspirated, but the /k/ of *scat* is not. However, in certain other languages, aspiration does make a difference to speakers and can result in distinct phonemes. We'll see that phonemes are psychological constructs that vary depending on a person's native language.

You now understand that the actual sounds of a language are something quite different from what is indicated by its alphabet and that the sounds of a language are related to each other in ways that alphabet gives no hint of, such as [p] and [b] are variations on the same operation (bilabial stop).

Armed with this, you are now in a position to understand one of the most basic, frequent, significant differences between the apparent and the actual in language. Namely, we generate words on two levels, according to a basic contrast that linguists have studied over the past hundred years: the *phonemic* versus the *phonetic*.

What is just a variation in one language is a "real sound" in others. To speakers of Hindi and Korean, for example, these two sounds sound as different as /p/ and /b/ do to English speakers, and the two sounds can make a difference in the meaning of a word. For instance, in Korean, /pʰal/ means "arm", while /pal/ means "foot". The same aspiration contrast exists for the other voiceless stops, /t/ and /k/.

tʰal	mask	kʰal	knife
tal	moon	kal	will go

43

Here compares /t/ and /d/ in Korean and English.

Phoneme	English	Sound/Allophone	Korean	Phoneme
/t/	[tʰæk] (tack)	[tʰ]	[tʰal] (mask)	/tʰ/
	[stæk] (stack)	[t]	[tal] (moon)	/t/
/d/	[dak] (dock)	[d]	[mandu] (dumpling)	

Another example of sounds that are phonemes in English but not in another language is /z/ and /s/. These two sounds are distinct phonemes in English but allophones in some varieties of Spanish. And in most dialects of English, /n/ and /ŋ/ are separate phonemes (as in *run* and *rung*), but in Italian and Spanish they are allophones. Many sound pairs are phonemes in other languages but not in English. Consider Lushootseed, for example, a Salish language spoken in the state of Washington. This language has a voiceless palatal affricate /č/ like English, but it also has an ejective version of that sound (a voiceless ejective palatal affricate) that is a distinct phoneme, so there are words that differ only in having /č/ instead of /č'/, and the two words mean different things: /č əɬ/ "we" and /č'əɬ/ "tear", for example.

3.4 Phonological Rules

From the discussion of phonemes versus allophones in last section, we know that the environment in which a sound occurs can affect the way it is produced. For example, voiceless stops that occur at the beginning of a stressed syllable are aspirated (as in *top* /tap/), and they are unaspirated when they occur in other positions (as in *stop* /stap/).

All of these elements in the sound system are governed by rules. Our main task in this lecture is to explore these **phonological rules** to understand how and why sounds affect each other and to understand our unconscious knowledge underlying these processes.

You've learnt how to distinguish and represent the sounds of English. When we speak, however, we don't utter each sound separately with a neat

3 Phonology

break in between. The word fact, for example, is not /f/ + /æ/ + /k/ + /t/; rather, each sound blends into the next. Sometimes that blending leads to neighbouring sounds affecting one another. When that happens, it does so in predictable and rule-governed ways. In this lecture we also examine aspects of phonology bigger than single sounds; we explore syllables, variation in pitch, and variation in loudness to understand how these processes can affect meaning and how and why the rules change and vary.

3.4.1 Assimilation Rules

One of the most common phonological rules across all languages is assimilation, the process of making one sound more like a neighbouring one with respect to some features. Here are some examples of assimilation.

Vowel Nasalization

When most English speakers say the word *man*, they begin to lower the velum so that air can pass through the nasal cavity for the /n/ while they are still saying the vowel /æ/. This opening of the velum has the effect of nasalizing the vowel, marked by ~ (pan/pæn/ as [pæ~n]).

This rule of nasalization in English holds for all vowels in that position. A vowel becomes nasalized when it precedes a nasal consonant (n,ŋ, or m).

Speakers of some dialects, especially those in the North-eastern United States and parts of the Midwest, have more nasalization (allow more air to pass through the nasal cavity and also to pass through earlier in the production of the vowel) than other speakers do.

Alveolar Nasal Assimilation

Many adults, especially in casual speech, and most children assimilate the place of articulation of the nasal to the following labial consonant in the word *sandwich* (sandwich /sænwɪč/ → /sæmwɪč/).

The alveolar nasal /n/ assimilates to the bilabial /w/ by changing the alveolar to a bilabial /m/. (The /d/ of the spelling is not present for most speakers, though it can occur in careful pronunciation.)

Nasal Assimilation

Nasal assimilation, one of the more common phonological processes found in natural languages, occurs when a nasal phoneme assimilates the place features of another consonant in its environment.

Another example of the assimilation of /n/ to what follows can be seen when the /n/ of a word like *can* (among others) can assimilate to the place of articulation of the following consonant. Compare the following:

> *I can be ready in five minutes. can be* /kæn bi/ → /kæm bi/
> *I can go with you. can go* /kæn go/ → /kæŋ go/

Sometimes we are so influenced by the spelling that we don't realize that such assimilation occurs, though it does for most English speakers in casual speech.

Palatalization

Palatalization is a common process that results from an interaction between either front vowels or a /y/ glide and a neighbouring alveolar consonant, resulting in a fricative or affricate palatal consonant. This phonological shift varies across dialects as well as across careful versus casual speech. For example,

> alveolar stop + high front vowel or glide→ palatalized fricative or affricate
> t + yu→ č *mature* /mə tyur/ → /mə čur/

Similarly, alveolar stops that are followed by /r/ become palatalized: d + r→ ǰr *drink*; t + r → čr *truck*.

These examples involve an across-the-board pronunciation shift; that is, because most speakers make these assimilations all the time, we can say that the language has changed. Native English speakers don't say /netiə n/ or /gresiə s/; rather they now say /nešən/ and /grešəs/, where the alveolars have become palatalized: t + i → š as in nation; s + i → š as in gracious.

Voicing Assimilation

Voicing assimilation occurs quite frequently in English. The following example shows how voiced /v/ of the word *have* assimilates to the voiceless /t/

3 Phonology

following it in the expression *have* to: /hæv tu/ → /hæf tu/.

The same assimilation happens in the /d/ of *used to*, which becomes /t/, and the /z/ of *has* in *has to*, which becomes /s/. In children's acquisition of language, assimilation is a very common process. One example of this process is assimilation of voiced sounds, so a word like paper with two voiceless /p/s may assimilate to the voicing of the neighbouring vowels, resulting in a pronunciation like: paper /bebə/.

The child changes the voiceless /p/s to voiced sounds to assimilate to the voiced vowels, resulting in voicing across the board. This also happens in adult variations. So, for some speakers (including adults), an /s/ between two vowels becomes voiced, resulting in /z/: *casserole* /kæsə rol/ → /kæzə rol/ ; *Leslie* /lɛsli/ → /lɛzli/.

In fact, much dialectal variation is a result of assimilation. Another example of this assimilation is that some speakers pronounce the word *thanks* with a voiced /ð/ rather than the voiceless /θ/: *thanks* /θæŋks/ → /ðæŋks/.

And sometimes the /k/ and /s/ may assimilate with respect to voicing as well, resulting in /ðæŋgz/ or *Thanksgiving* /ðæŋgzɪvɪŋ/.

Voicing assimilation is at work in the production of the English regular plural ending *-s*. The inflection *-s* in English occurs in three contexts: as a third person singular present tense verb form (takes), as a plural marker on nouns (dishes), and as a marker of possession (man's). But while each inflection is spelled as *-s* or *-es*, the inflections have three different pronunciations. Two of the pronunciations, [s] and [z], are the result of voicing assimilation between the consonant ending the base to which these inflections are attached and the inflections themselves. If the base ends with a voiced consonant or a vowel (all vowels in English are voiced), then the inflection will be voiced [z]: *feels* [fiəlz].

If the stem ends with a voiceless consonant, the inflection will be voiceless:*walks* [wɔks]; *fights* [faits].

With stems ending with the consonants /s/, /z/, /ʃ/, /tʃ/, and /d/, neither [s] nor [z] is possible, since a consonant cluster such as [ss] or [zz] is not possible in English. As a result, it is necessary to insert an [i] or [ə] between the consonant-ended stem and the inflection [z]:*hisses* [hisiz] or [hisəz]; *fizzes* [fiziz].

3.4.2 Dissimilation Rules

Rules of dissimilation cause two neighbouring sounds to become less alike with respect to some features.

Dissimilation of Liquids and Nasal Sounds

Historically, Latin *turtur* was borrowed into English, but the second /r/ changed to /l/. Latin *purpura* and Middle English *purpre* became *purple* in Present-Day English (turtur → turtle; purpre → purple).

Consider a similar example of dissimilation of liquid consonants that took place when the suffix *-al* was attached to some Latin nouns to make adjectives. The regular suffixation process gives us pairs like the following: *orbit/orbital, person/personal, culture/cultural, electric/electrical*. However, when an /l/ precedes the ending anywhere in the root, the ending is changed from *-al* to *-ar* as a result of dissimilation: *single/singular, module/modular, luna/lunar*.

Latin *marmor* became Present-Day English marble via two ways of dissimilation: the second *r* changed to *l*, then the second *m* changed to *b*, to dissimilate the two bilabial nasals, /m/ (marmor → marmle → marble).

Dissimilation of Fricative Sounds

Many speakers avoid neighbouring fricatives by changing one to a different place of articulation, so a word like *months* /mʌnθs/ becomes /mʌnts/, in which the fricative /θ/ becomes /t/. This happens frequently in casual speech and can disappear in more careful speech (Also, the /t/ here may be assimilating to the same alveolar place of articulation as the preceding /n/, so perhaps both assimilation and dissimilation are at work.).

3.4.3 Insertion Rules

Rules of **insertion** (also called *epenthesis*) cause a segment absent at the phonemic level to be added to the phonetic form of a word.

Insertion of Vowels

From Old English to Middle English, vowels were inserted between consonants in certain positions. These insertions are indicated in these Middle

3 Phonology

English spellings.

Old English		Middle English	Present-Day English
þurh*	→	thorow	"thorough"
setl	→	setel	"seat"
æfre	→	ever	"dream"

*The þ is a symbol used in Old English to represent the interdental fricatives /θ/ and /ð/.

In present-day English, many variations across dialects involve insertion (or not) of vowels. Do you have a vowel in *realtor* between the /l/ and the /t/? Often, too, a vowel is inserted between the consonants of a consonant cluster, as an /ə/ occurs between /p/ and /l/ in words like *paraplegic* or *quadriplegic*.

Insertion of Consonants

Another example of an insertion that happened during the Middle English period is the insertion of /d/ in what now appears as *thunder* (The <þ> is an Old English symbol representing /ð/ in this word.).

Old English *þunor* → Present-Day English *thunder*
(compare German Donner 'thunder')

The alveolar stop with the same place of articulation as the nasal /n/ (alveolar) was inserted in Old English speakers' speech to ease transition to the vowel. This /d/ was also inserted into the spelling and eventually became the standard spelling. The *d* in Present-Day English *thunder* is no longer considered as an insertion for current speakers, as it is present phonemically.

Insertion of Voiceless Stops

A common insertion takes place between a nasal and a voiceless fricative when a voiceless stop with the same place of articulation as the nasal is inserted.

hamster /hæmstrɪ/ → /hæmpstrɪ/

something /sʌmθɪŋ/ → /sʌmpθɪŋ/ or /sʌmpθɪn/*
or
/sʌmθɪn/
strength /strɛŋθ/ → /strɛŋkθ/

*Note the further deletion and assimilation that can occur in this word's pronunciation: /sʌmpmɪ/

This insertion rule also led to the two common spellings of the surname *Thomson/Thompson*. Both derive from the English and Scottish first name *Thomas*. The *p* was inserted in the spelling by some people because it sounds as if it is there (And remember, it's *Chomsky*, not *Chompsky*!). The word *empty* underwent this insertion process; in Old English the word was *æmtig*, with no /p/ between the /m/ and the /t/.

Insertion of /y/

In some dialects of English—most British dialects and some southeastern American dialects—a /y/ is inserted between initial alveolar consonants and preceding high vowels, so words like *news, Tuesday*, and *duke* are pronounced /nyuz/, /tyuzde/, and /dyuk/. This insertion—which used to be the norm in American English (so maybe it's not insertion but is better described as deletion)—appears to be gradually on its way out of the language, with the /y/ disappearing when following certain kinds of consonants, as in *news*, but not yet lost in others, like *few*, /fyu/, and *puny*, /pyuni/.

3.4.4 Deletion Rules

Rules of deletion cause a segment present at the phonemic level to be deleted at the phonetic level of a word.

Deletion of /r/ after Vowels

In many English dialects, /r/ is deleted when it follows a vowel. So, words like *car* and *yard* are pronounced like /ka/ and /yad/. The dropping of /r/s in words like *car, park, hard*, and *court* is usually perceived as somewhat nonstandard in American English. It occurs most frequently in some dialects of New England and some dialects of the Deep South. However, in Britain, the dropping of /r/s in the very same words is considered characteristic of the standard dialect and viewed favourably not only by British speakers but also by

3 Phonology

most American English speakers. This contrast in the attitude toward the same linguistic feature illustrates that standard and nonstandard features of dialects are socially, not linguistically, determined.

Deletion of Fricative Next to Fricative

The same process that leads to dissimilation can lead instead to deletion of one of the similar sounds. For example, in words like *fifths* /fɪfθs/ and *sixths* /sɪksθs/, in which three fricatives occur in a row, one or two of them frequently are deleted: /fɪfθs/ → /fɪfs/ or /fɪθs/ or even /fɪs/.

Deletion of Similar Sounds or Syllables

Repeated consonants or entire syllables containing similar sounds are often deleted in casual speech: probably /prabəbli/ → /prabli/ ; mirror /mɪrər/ → /mɪr/.

3.4.5 Fronting Rules

Fronting rules cause a segment produced in the back of the mouth to change to a segment produced at the front of the mouth. There are more front consonants than back consonants in the languages across the world, and front consonants are acquired before back consonants in most children's language.

Fronting of Velar Nasal to Alveolar Nasal

In many speakers' casual speech, words ending in *-ing* are pronounced with /ɪn/ rather than /ɪŋ/. The velar nasal has fronted to become an alveolar nasal: running /rʌnɪŋ/ → /rʌnɪn/.

Fronting in Child Language

Many children front most velar sounds during the first few years of language acquisition: goat /got/ → /dot/ ; OK /oke/ → /ote/.

Fronting of /x/

A historical example of velar fronting is the velar fricative /x/ becoming a labiodental fricative /f/ in words such as *tough* and *enough*. The letters *h* and later *gh* were used to represent the velar fricative /x/ in Old English. In some modern English words that formerly had /x/, the consonant was fronted to /f/, but in others it disappeared completely (*though, bough, night,* etc.).

3.4.6 Exchange Rules

Exchange rules reorder sounds or syllables. This exchange process is also known as metathesis.

Exchanging /s/ and a Consonant

The two consonants /s/ and /k/ switched around in English. The same process that leads to the much-stigmatized, metathesized pronunciation of *ask* also occurs in the less-stigmatized pronunciation of *asterisk: asterisk* /æstərɪsk/ → /æstərɪks/.

Exchanging /r/ and a Vowel

Another common kind of metathesis occurs in /r/ and a neighbouring vowel. This can be seen in current dialect variation, in historical examples, and in child language:

Old English		**Present-Day English**
brid	→	bird
drit	→	dirt
thridda	→	third

Modern English dialect variations include metathesized versions of children as /čɪldərn/ and pretty as /pərti/, and the more common /ɪntərdus/ for /ɪntrədus/ "introduce".

Exchanging Syllable Onsets

The onsets (beginning consonants or consonant clusters) of syllables commonly metathesize. This manipulation of the first sounds of syllables is especially common in child language, as in these common examples.

animal	/ænɪməl/	→	/æmɪnəl/
cinnamon	/sɪnəmən/	→	/sɪmənən/

Such metatheses are also at work in adult language. The pronunciation of *nuclear* as /nukyələr/ involves metathesis, perhaps.

3.4.7 Multiple-Rule Processes

Sometimes more than one phonological process is employed in a phonological variation or change. Consider the following example, which involves both deletion and assimilation: *pumpkin* /pʌmpkɪn/ → /pʌŋkɪn/.

The second /p/ deletes (as a result of dissimilation) and then the /m/ assimilates to the same place of articulation (velar) as the following /k/.

Another example is the word something: *something* /sʌmθɪŋ/ or /sʌmθɪn/ → /sʌmpθɪŋ/ or /sʌmpθɪn/.

When the word is pronounced in casual speech as /sʌmpmʊ/, there is not only insertion of /p/ (discussed previously) but also assimilation (of the /n/ to /m/) and deletion (of /θ/).

It's not always clear why exactly a phonological process has taken place. Sometimes the rules aren't easily motivated by a process. For example, in some dialects of English in the United States (in the South, parts of the Midwest, and more recently, parts of the West), the vowel /ɛ/ has become /ɪ/ when it occurs before a nasal consonant, /m/, /n/, or /ŋ/.

wren   /rɪn/
pen   /pɪn/
gem   /jɪm/
temper   /tɪmpər/
length   /lɪŋθ/
strength /strɪŋθ/

Though this is a rule-governed process—we can see that the vowel changes only when a nasal follows—it's not entirely clear what it is about the nasal that leads to the vowel change.

In this section, you have seen how phonological variation and language change are motivated by the same kinds of natural phonological processes. You should be aware that the variety of rules introduced here is not exhaustive and that the set of rules can vary across dialects and even among individuals—each person has a slightly different set of phonological rules and processes in his or her speech.

The stigmatization is stronger for consonant variation primarily because the consonant sounds correlate more directly with spelling than vowel sounds. Though the motivation behind most of these phonological processes is **ease of articulation**—that is, making something easier to say—that motivation is always competing with other factors. If ease of articulation were the sole motivation for language change, then presumably we would all be moving toward the same kinds of changes, not only in English but in other languages. Also, it is an ongoing area of research among phoneticians and phonologists to discover the motivation for phonological processes in general.

3.5 Suprasegmentals

In this section, we will explore some aspects of phonology bigger than the single sound, the "segment"; these are called suprasegmentals, and they include syllables, stress, and intonation.

The study of suprasegmentals extends the focus of inquiry to units that are larger than individual segments—syllables, words, phrases, and clauses—and to the features of sound that describe these units, specifically stress and intonation. Of key importance to both stress and intonation is the notion of the syllable.

3.5.1 Syllables

A syllable consists of three parts: an onset, a nucleus, and a coda.

It is actually difficult to provide a neat definition of a syllable, though we all have awareness of syllables naturally and unconsciously. Very young children are able to tap out syllables; many phonological processes refer to the syllables of words; and children (and adults) manipulate syllables quite skilfully in all sorts of ways.

Structure of Syllables

Languages have varying syllable structures. The group of consonants at the beginning of a syllable is called the **onset**, and the vowel and any consonants following it at the end of the syllable are called the **rime**. The symbol traditionally used by linguists for a syllable is the Greek letter sigma, σ.

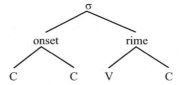

The rime can be further divided into a **nucleus**, a vowel that is the heart of the rime, and a **coda**, the consonant(s) at the end of the rime.

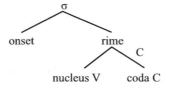

Vowels are almost always the nucleus of a syllable. However, if the syllable lacks a vowel, certain consonants are able to take over as the nucleus of the syllable. In English, an onset can consist of a cluster of consonants. Certain groups of two phonemes can occur next to each other at the beginning of a syllable: /fl/, /sp/, and /tr/, among others. Three sounds can occur as the onset of a syllable in English: /spl/, /spr/, /skr/, /str/, and the rare /skl/, as in *sclerosis*. You must remember to ignore spelling when considering cluster combinations and focus on only the sounds (so *thistle* and *psychology*, for example, do not contain word-initial consonant clusters, even though they are spelled with initial consonants).

Learning and Research Resources

- *Oxford Bibliographies*—Syllables
https://www.oxfordbibliographies.com/view/document/obo-9780199772810/obo-9780199772810-0084.xml?rskey=CJE6VK&result=1&q=syllables#firstMatch

Oxford Bibliographies offers exclusive, authoritative research guides. It combines the best features of an annotated bibliography and a high-level encyclopaedia, which directs researchers to the best available scholarship across a wide variety of subjects. Can you use *Oxford Bibliographies* to find some studies about ***Syllables***?

3.5.2 Phonotactics

Note that all the consonant clusters just discussed must occur in a particular order and in a particular position within the syllable. Although /spl/ may occur at the beginning of a syllable, /pls/ cannot. And though /spl/ may occur as the onset of a syllable, it may not occur as the coda of a syllable. Such restrictions are known **asphonotactics**, a branch of phonology that deals with natural and unconscious restrictions on the permissible combinations of phonemes in a particular language. English, for example, may have /ŋ/ at the end of a syllable as the coda but not as the onset: sing /sɪŋ/ */ŋɪs/ (* indicates an impossible word).

On the other hand, /kt/ is a possible coda, as in *kicked* /kɪkt/, but not a possible onset. We are quite aware of these restrictions as speakers of a language, as evidenced by our knowledge of the related **graphotactic** constraints (as these use letters, not sounds) of anagrams or jumbles, like those typically found in many newspapers and other word game collections. So, it doesn't take most people long to unscramble the letters irgn to make a word. We know that "ng" is not a possible combination at the beginning of the word or in the middle, so we quickly come up with *ring* or *grin*, rather than randomly trying the many possible combinations of the letters. Even slips of the tongue reveal our knowledge of phonotactic constraints. Consider the following intended and actual utterance pair:

scratching Daddy's back/skræčɪŋ dædiz/
snatching graddy's back /snæčɪŋ grædiz/

In this example, the /kr/ of *scratching* and the /d/ of *Daddy* exchange. However, since /sd/ is not a possible combination in English, the alveolar stop /d/ becomes the alveolar nasal /n/, which is the only voiced alveolar allowed to follow /s/; thus /skr/ has become /sn/, and the velar /k/ that is now in initial position in the second word becomes the voiced velar /g/. So even when we mess up, we do not violate our language's phonotactic constraints.

The rime in English can consist of a vowel followed by a consonant, as in *bat* /bæt/, or a cluster of two consonants, as in *toast*, *lift*, and *kicked* /kɪkt/; three consonants, as in *wasps* /wasps/; or even four, as in *prompts* /prampts/ or *sixths*

/sɪksθs/. Despite English allowing syllables with complex onsets and codas, speakers often tend to reduce those clusters. Consider the /rst/ of the word *first* in a compound word like *first grade,* which typically is pronounced /fʌrs gred/ rather than /fʌrst gred/, and the cluster in *sixths* /sɪksθs/, which most speakers would reduce to /sɪks/ except in careful speech. In many dialects of English, including African American English and Navajo English, word-final consonant clusters are reduced, so words such as *desk, toast,* and *walked* are pronounced /dɛs/, /tos/, and /wak/. This phenomenon is sensitive to morphological information, so if the cluster reduction would eliminate a grammatical marker, such as past-tense information, *-ed*, then it is less common. For example, the reduced form of the past tense *walked* would be /wak/, which would be the same form as the present tense *walk* /wak/, and thus such a reduction is less common.

3.5.3 Stress

Stress refers to the relative prominence or emphasis of certain syllables in a word. This prominence can be achieved in several ways, depending on the language. Stress is usually produced by an increase in articulatory force, by an increase in the airflow, and sometimes by increased muscular tension in the articulators.

All English words will contain one syllable that has primary stress: a syllable that is more prominent than the other syllables in the word. In the word *happy*, for instance, the primary stress falls on the first syllable because of the two syllables in this word, and the first syllable is more prominent than the second syllable: *'ha.ppy*. Some words contain syllables with varying degrees of stress. As was noted in the last chapter, compound words in English are marked by a specific stress pattern: primary stress on the first element and secondary stress on the second element, as in *'headlight*. However, the extent to which English words consistently exhibit varying degrees of stress is a controversial notion. As a result, most discussions of word stress in English focus mainly on primary stress.

Stress has several different functions in English. In the first place, it can be used in sentences to give special emphasis to a word or to contrast one word with another. As we have seen, even a word such as *and* can be given a contrastive stress. The contrast can be implicit rather than explicit. For example, if someone else says, or if you even thought that someone else might possibly say (using stress marks within regular orthography):

'John or 'Mary should 'go.
You might, without any prior context actually spoken, say:

'I think 'John 'and 'Mary should 'go.

Another major function of stress in English is to indicate the syntactic category of a word. There are many noun-verb oppositions, such as an '*insult, to in'sult; an 'overflow, to over 'flow; an 'increase, to in 'crease.* In these three pairs of words, the noun has the stress on the first syllable and the verb has it on the last. The placement of the stress indicates the syntactic category of the word. (Of course, there are nouns with second-syllable stress—like *gui'tar, pi'ano, and trom'bone*—and verbs with first-syllable stress—like to *'tremble,* to *'flutter*, and to *'simper*—so stress placement is not determined by syntactic category but is simply a cue in certain noun–verb pairs as to the identity of the word.)

Similar oppositions occur in cases where two-word phrases form compounds, such as a *'walkout,* to *'walk 'out*; a *'put-on,* to *'put 'on*; a *'pushover,* to *'push 'over*. In these cases, there is a stress only on the first element of the compound for the nouns but on both elements for the verbs. Stress also has a syntactic function in distinguishing between a compound noun, such as a *'hot dog* (a form of food), and an adjective followed by a noun, as in the phrase a *'hot 'dog* (an overheated animal). Compound nouns have a single stress on the first element, and the adjective-plus-noun phrases have stresses on both elements.

Many other variations in stress can be associated with the grammatical structure of the words. Table 3.1 exemplifies the kinds of alternations that can occur. All the words in the first column have the main stress on the first syllable. When the noun-forming suffix "-y" occurs, the stress in these words shifts to the second syllable. But as you can see in the third column, the adjectival suffix "-ic" moves the stress to the syllable immediately preceding it, which in these words is on the third syllable. If you make a sufficiently complex set of rules, it is possible to predict the location of the stress in the majority of English words. There are very few examples of lexical items such as *differ* and *defer* that have the same syntactic function (they are both verbs) but different stress patterns. Below are another pair of words illustrating that differences in stress are not always differences between nouns and verbs.

Table 3.1   English word stress alternations

ˈ _ _ _	_ ˈ _ _ _	_ _ ˈ _ _
diplomat	diplomacy	diplomatic
photograph	photography	photographic
monotone	monotony	monotonic

In some longer words, it may seem as if there is more than one stressed syllable. For example, say the word *multiplication* and try to tap on the stressed syllables. You will find that you can tap on the first and the fourth syllables— ˈmultipliˈcation. The fourth syllable seems to have a higher degree of stress. The same is true of other long words, such as ˈmagnifiˈcation and ˈpycholinˈguistics. But this apparently higher degree of stress on the later syllable occurs only when the word is said in isolation or at the end of a phrase. Try saying a sentence such as *The ˈpsycholinˈguistics ˈcourse was ˈfun*. If you tap on each stressed syllable, you will find that there is no difference between the first and fourth syllables of psycholinguistics. If you have a higher degree of stress on the fourth syllable in psycholinguistics, this word will be given a special emphasis, as though you were contrasting some other psychology courses with a psycholinguistics course. The same is true of the word *magnification* in a sentence such as *The deˈgree of ˈmagnifiˈcation deˈpends on the ˈlens*. The word *magnification* will not have a larger stress on the fourth syllable as long as you do not break the sentence into two parts and leave this word at the end of a phrase.

Learning and Research Resources

- **English Club—Word Stress Rules**
https://www.englishclub.com/pronunciation/word-stress-rules.htm
English Club is a free website which provides many useful English

language learning resources. This link will help you understand the word stress in English, and you can find some recordings.

- **15.ai**

https://15.ai/

15.ai is an AI text-to-speech tool for generating voices of various characters. The voices are generated in real time using multiple audio synthesis algorithms and customized neural networks trained on very little available data. This project demonstrates not only a significant reduction in the amount of audio required to realistically clone voices while retaining their affective prosodies, but also the feasibility of an on-demand, stable, and autonomously-improving speech synthesis application that aims to mimic a voice of limited availability. It might be useful for you to analyse the phonological features of different people or ….

3.5.4 Intonation

In the previous chapter on phonetics, tone—variation in pitch—is discussed. Some languages can vary the pitch of a syllable, and this variation can result in meaning differences; Putonghua and Nupe examples were given. Varying the pitch across a longer stretch of speech is known as **intonation**. Many languages, including English, use such pitch variations to convey surprise, irony, and questioning. American English typically has rising intonation across the utterance for what are called *yes-no* questions (*"She bought a new car?"*) and falling intonation for information-seeking questions (also called *wh-* questions) (*"What does she want to buy?"*), although there is much variation of these patterns in both American and British dialects. Stress and intonation can interact at the sentence level; word-level stress patterns and pitch can be modified to indicate which part of the sentence is in focus or which word should receive special emphasis. In English, new and important information is typically placed at the end of a clause; therefore, utterance stress, when used neutrally—what we consider "normal" intonation contour—is usually associated with the end of a clause. In the following sentence, "neutral" intonation means that the utterance stress does not make any major changes in the interpretation of the sentence: *Three children were sitting on the grey couch.*

In any given utterance, one stressed syllable stands out as most prominent.

This stressed syllable is called the **intonation nucleus** (not to be confused with the nucleus of a syllable). This intonation nucleus can be moved and result in meaning changes; thus, the phonological system interacts with meaning, the semantic system. Consider the change in meaning when various other words of the utterance receive more stress (In these examples, the capitalized words indicate the intonation nucleus. They receive primary utterance stress and accompany higher pitch.).

(a) Three CHILDREN (not women, elves, men, etc.) were sitting on the blue couch.

(b) Three children were sitting on the blue COUCH (not the chair, steps, etc.).

(c) Three children were sitting on the BLUE (not the purple, gray, black, etc.) couch.

Contrastive stress like that indicated by these examples rejects something and suggests that what is being rejected has been already introduced into the discourse or is implied. There is evidence that intonational contours and patterns are stored in a distinct part of the brain from the rest of language. When someone experiences brain damage to the left side of the brain that seriously affects their linguistic abilities, making them unable to produce fluent or grammatical speech, they often maintain the appropriate intonation patterns of their language. When right-hemisphere damage takes place, the result may be that the patient speaks with a monotone. And when babies who have not yet acquired any words begin to babble at around 6 months of age, they often utter nonsense syllables using the appropriate intonation pattern of the language they are acquiring.

Group-Work Activities

"I daily examine myself on three points: whether, in transacting business for others, I may have been not faithful; whether, in intercourse with friends, I may have been not sincere; whether I may have not mastered and practiced the instructions of my teacher."

吾日三省吾身:"为人谋而不忠乎？与朋友交而不信乎？传不习乎？"

The Master said, "The virtuous will be sure to speak correctly, but those whose speech is good may not always be virtuous. Men of principle are sure to be bold, but those who are bold may not always be men of principle."

子曰:"有德者必有言。有言者不必有德。仁者必有勇。勇者不必有仁。"

The Master said, "Some men of worth retire from the world. Some retire from particular states. Some retire because of disrespectful looks. Some retire because of contradictory language."

子曰:"贤者辟世,其次辟地,其次辟色,其次辟言。"

1. Can you find the stress in these sentences?
2. What is the intonation nucleus in these sentences?
3. Do you agree that we need to reflect on ourselves regularly?
4. How do you understand the statement that "The virtuous will be sure to speak correctly, but those whose speech is good may not always be virtuous"?
5. Why is it that "Some retire because of contradictory language"?

Summary

The study of sound, however, is also suprasegmental: it extends beyond single phonemes to syllables, words, phrases, and clauses. All words in English contain one or more syllables, and one of these syllables will carry the primary stress. Intonation also serves to segment speech into grammatical structures, though the correspondence between grammar and intonation is closer in more carefully prepared speech than in spontaneous dialogues.

Learning Highlights: Read and Think—Linguistics and Life

Phonological system has universality. Since there are few absolute universals such as "all languages have stops" and "all languages have at least two degrees of vowel height", theory-driven or "architectural" universals concerning distinctive features and syllable structure are also considered. (Hyman, 2008)

3 Phonology

"有声语言或词的语言始终是人类社会唯一能作人们完善的交际工具的语言。"——斯大林《马克思主义和语言学问题——答同志们》

Research Fronts

● Alejandrina Cristia, Amanda Seidl and Alexander L. Francis from Purdue University did a research about phonological features in infancy. Their study shows that

...young infants may use abstract phonological features to learn sound patterns. However, changes in the ability to learn patterns involving features becomes more constrained with development and language experience. Furthermore, research on toddlers' ability to learn minimal pairs is initially limited. Given the lack of overlap between the ability to learn sound patterns based on features and the ability to learn a pair of words differing in a single feature, we argue for the separation of the classificatory and the distinctive function...

(View the latest issues about phonology at https://www.cambridge.org/core/journals/phonology/latest-issue)

Self-Study Activities

1. Can you tell the difference between phonetics and phonology?
2. Can you transfer the following phonetics to a text? For example, /tʃaɪˈniːz kəˈlɪgrəfi rɪˈfɜːz tu ˈraɪtɪŋ ɑːt ənd tekˈniːks wɪð ˈraɪtɪŋ ˈbrʌʃɪz/. is Chinese calligraphy refers to writing art and techniques with writing brushes.

(1) <ˈgʌnpaʊdə ɪz əˈnʌð ər ˌeɪnʃənt tʃaɪˈniːz ɪnˈvenʃn̩>

(2) <ðə raɪz ənd set əv ˈsʌn ˌriːprɪˈzents həʊp ɪn ðə hɑːts əv tʃaɪˈniːz ˈpiːpl̩>

(3) <ə raʊnd muːn ˌriːprɪˈzents ˈfæmli ˌriːˈjuːnɪən ənd ˈɒfnrɪˈmaɪndz ˈpiːpl̩ əv ðeə ˈfæmli>

(4) <ˈkærəktəz wə kɑːvd ɒn iːtʃ piːs əv kleɪ wɪtʃ ˈlʊkt laɪk ðə siːlz ˈwaɪdli juːst ɪn tʃaɪnə>

3. Indicate which syllable in the words below carries the primary stress.
(1) recitation (2) predominate (3) cigarette (4) contest
(5) bureau (6) contentment (7) dislike (8) unconvincing

4. What are the functions of stress in English language?

5. Read aloud the following paragraph with your partner. Pay attention to your pronunciation and intonation.

Peking Opera, is an ancient performance art with a history of 200 years. Peking Opera has four kinds of roles according to different identities and personalities. The lyrics of Peking Opera are performed with swinging or rhythmic speaking, accompanied by dozens of musical instruments. Now, Peking Opera still enchants many Chinese people and foreigners with its unique charm.

6. Can you analyse the stress in the following sentence? How does the variation of stress influence the meaning of the sentence? Please discuss in group and share your ideas with each other.

冬天冷的时候，能穿多少就穿多少；
夏天热的时候，能穿多少就穿多少。

Further Reading

Randolf Quirk et al's *A Comprehensive Grammar of the English Language* (London: Longman, 1985) provides an overview of tone units and their relationship with grammar (pp. 1355–1375).

A more general overview of English intonation can be found in Paul Tench's *The Intonation Systems of English* (London: Cassell, 1996).

To learn how to transcribe intonation in sentences, please read Peter Ladefoged and Keith Johnson's *A Course in Phonetics* (6 ed.).

Outline

Ⅰ. Phonology is the study of the sound system and the processes we use to discover the unconscious systems underlying our speech.
　A. Phonetics is a discipline that studies production, transmission and

3 Phonology

reception of speech sounds.

B. Phonemics is a discipline that studies the sounds and sound patterns of a specific language.

Ⅱ. In linguistic terms, "real sounds" are *phonemes*. The other sounds are *allophones* of a phoneme.

A. **Phoneme** is a basic unit of sound that is able to distinguish one word from another in a given language. (It can be used to contrast meaning.) This is different from a letter. (A letter is a unit of writing, not speech.)

B. **Minimal pairs:** words that differ by only a single phoneme in the same position of a word.

C. **Allophones**, although often represented by one letter of the alphabet, are quite central to how we express sounds. An allophone is one of two or more variants of the same phoneme in a language. It doesn't change meanings. For example, because there are many allophones of the phoneme /l/, the word oil actually sounds virtually identical when played backward.

Ⅲ. You learned that the environment in which a sound occurs can affect the way it is produced. We learned some phonological rules to understand how and why sounds affect each other and to understand our unconscious knowledge underlying these processes.

A. Assimilation rules: the process of making one sound more like a neighbouring one with respect to some feature.

　ⅰ) Vowel nasalization
　ⅱ) Alveolar nasal assimilation
　ⅲ) Nasal assimilation
　ⅳ) Palatalization
　ⅴ) Voicing assimilation

B. Dissimilation rules

C. Insertion rules: rules of **insertion** cause a segment not present at the phonemic level to be added to the phonetic form of a word.

　ⅰ) Vowels
　ⅱ) Consonants
　ⅲ) Voiceless stops
　ⅳ) /y/

D. Deletion rules: rules of **deletion** cause a segment present at the phonemic level to be deleted at the phonetic level of a word.

ⅰ) /r/ after vowels
ⅱ) Fricative next to fricative
ⅲ) Similar sounds or syllables
ⅳ) Consonants clusters
ⅴ) Syllable-final consonants clusters

E. Fronting rules: rules of **fronting** cause a segment produced in the back of the mouth to change to a segment produced at the front of the mouth.
ⅰ) Fronting of velar nasal to alveolar nasal
ⅱ) Child language
ⅲ) /x/

F. Exchange rules
ⅰ) Exchanging /s/ and a consonant
ⅱ) Exchanging /r/ and a vowel
ⅲ) Exchanging syllable onsets

Ⅳ. Suprasegmental: The study of suprasegmentals extends the focus of inquiry to units that are larger than individual segments—syllables, words, phrases, and clauses—and to the features of sound that describe these units, specifically stress and intonation.

A. Syllable: Languages have varying syllable structures. The group of consonants at the beginning of a syllable is called the **onset**, and the vowel and any consonants following it at the end of the syllable are called the **rime**. The rime can be further divided into a **nucleus**, a vowel that is the heart of the rime, and a **coda**, the consonant(s) at the end of the rime.

B. Phonotactics: All the consonant clusters just discussed must occur in a particular order and in a particular position within the syllable.

C. Stress: the relative prominence or emphasis of certain syllables in a word.

D. Intonation: Varying the pitch across a longer stretch of speech is known as **intonation**.

4 Morphology

4.1 Introduction

This chapter focuses on words: their internal structure and the ways that linguists and lexicographers (those who create dictionaries) have studied their meaning. It starts with a definition of morphology, then continues with a description of the morpheme, the smallest unit of meaning, and how various kinds of morphemes are combined to create words. The remaining sections describe two different types of morphological process: derivation and inflection.

The study of how morphemes come together to make words is called **morphology**. Morphology includes the study of the system of rules underlying our knowledge of the structure of words; the word *morphology* is from the Greek words *morph-* "form/structure" and *-logy* (study). Morphology is closely linked to the study of our mental dictionary, or lexicon. The operations and systems we use to form words are called **word formation rules or lexical rules**. In practice, morphology focuses most upon morphemes that serve as tools of grammar, i.e. marking tense, changing words of one part of speech into another, or changing the meaning of words, rather than the morphemes that just describe an action or a person, place, or thing.

4.2 Morphemes

Just as the actual sounds are termed phonemes, actual units of meaning are termed **morphemes**. A morpheme is the smallest abstract linguistic unit that serves to carry meaning (not the smallest unit of meaning). The most basic elements in a language are its sounds. The next level upward is morpheme. A word may contain just one morpheme, such as *dog*, or more than one morpheme. For example, *hunter* contains two morphemes: *hunt* and the suffix *-er* that indicates someone performing an action. *Hunters* contains three, and *unthinkingly* four morphemes.

4.2.1 Roots

Not all morphemes are equally central to the formation of a word. Morphemes are of two main types: **roots** and **affixes**. We turn our attention first to roots. Every word has at least one root. Roots are at the center of word-derivational processes. They carry the basic meaning from which the rest of the sense of the word can be derived. Morphemes such as *chair, green, ballet, father, cardigan, America, Mississippi,* are roots; these roots also happen to be free forms, i.e., independent words. But more often, roots, like *seg* in *segment, gen* in *genetics, card* in *cardiac, sequ* in *sequence, brev* in *brevity, pter* in *pterodactyl,* cannot stand alone as words. They are called **bound root morphemes**, as distinct from **free root morphemes** (the ones that are also independent words).

Most bound roots found in the language today are of classical origin, i.e., they were borrowed into English from Latin or Greek during the Renaissance, or through French. Moreover, we usually borrow words from these languages wholesale, i.e., the classical roots came into the language nested inside derived forms such as *segment, genetics, cardiacs,* etc. Sometimes, though not very frequently, borrowed roots do make their way into the inventory of free forms too, for example, *contra* in the meaning of "counterrevolutionary" (1981), and *graph* (1878), *phone* (1866) are some examples. As you can see from the dates of their first recorded appearance in English, such roots which are also independent words are fairly recent and formed by shortening the classical words or phrases that contain them, i.e., their transition from bound to free roots has occurred on English soil. So, it would be fair to say that roots borrowed from classical sources are nearly always bound roots.

On the other hand, the number of bound roots of Germanic origin like *hap(p)* "luck, fortune," as in *hapless, happy,* is comparatively small. Of Germanic origin are the bound roots of *feckless, reckless, ruthless, listless, uncouth, unkempt.* What has happened in all these cases is a straight forward historical change: a root, which used to be also a word at earlier times, became

4 Morphology

obsolete or disappeared completely, leaving behind only a derivative. Thus, *feckless* is derived from a sixteenth-century Scots word *feck*, a shortened form of *effect*. Later *effect* was reintroduced into Scots, replacing the form *feck*, yet its derivative *feckless* "ineffective" is still around. We consider *ruth* in *ruthless* as a bound morpheme today, but it used to be a common word in English meaning "pity, sorrow" in the eighteenth century. Though it appears as an entry in many dictionaries, the word is obsolete in present-day English, but note its connection with the verb "to rue," from which the noun was obviously derived originally. In any case, the historical processes we are illustrating here are not recoverable without the aid of specialized dictionaries. For the ordinary speaker of English *feck-, hap(p)-, ruth-,* etc. are bound roots.

Bound root morphemes require that another morpheme be attached to them. This additional morpheme may be either another root or an affix. If it is another root, the result is a **compound**. Some issues related to compounds and compounding were discussed in Chapter 1. You will remember that words like *airship, birdcage, bookmark, flagship, hemisphere, hydrogen, phonograph, polymath, telephone,* etc. are compounds. They all contain two roots. If a bound root is not attached to another root, as in ***brev**ity,* ***cap**able,* ***card**iac,* ***gent**ile,* etc., it must be accompanied by an **affix**.

Affixes carry very little of the core meaning of a word. Mainly affixes have the effect of slightly modifying the meaning of the stem—a stem is either a root or a root plus an affix, or more than one root with or without affixes— to which more affixes can be attached. The most common modification is to change the word-class, the part of speech, to which the word belongs. Thus *child* (a noun) becomes an adjective in *childish*. That adjective can in turn be changed to an adverb: *childishly*, or to a different kind of noun, an "abstract" noun, by adding another affix, as in *childishness*. This process, known as *affixation*, is one of the two most fundamental processes in word formation (the other is compounding, discussed below). Let us therefore examine more closely the properties of affixes.

4.2.2 Affixes

All morphemes which are not roots are affixes. Affixes differ from roots in three ways.

- They do not form words by themselves; they have to be added to a stem.
- Their meanings, in many instances, are not as clear and specific as those of roots, and many of them are almost completely meaningless.
- Compared with the total number of roots, which is very large (thousands or tens of thousands in any language), the number of affixes is relatively small (a few hundred at most).

In English, all the productive affixes ("productive" in the sense that they do a lot of work) are either attached at the end of the stem, i. e. **suffixes**, or at the front of the stem, i. e. **prefixes**. Here are examples of common prefixes where the meaning is clear:

co + occur "occur together"	**peri** + meter "measure around"
mid + night "middle of the night"	**re** + turn "turn back"
mis + treat "treat badly"	**un** + filled "not filled"

And here are examples of common suffixes where the meaning is also clear:

act + **ion** "state of acting"	child + **ish** "like a child"
act + **or** "person who acts"	child + **hood** "state of being a child"
act + **ive** "pertaining to being in action"	child + **less** "without a child"

The majority of affixes are, unfortunately, less clear than these. We will provide more detailed information about them later, matching them to some of the possible meanings they may have.

All affixes, by definition, are bound morphemes. Historically it is quite normal for free morphemes to lose their independence and become "bound." One transparent example is the suffix *-less*: its origin in the adjective *less* "devoid of" and its connection with the word *less* do not require specialized knowledge. The suffixes *-dom*, *-hood*, and *-ship* once had independent meaning as nouns. *Dom* meant "doom, judgment, statute" and is the ancestor of the modern word *doom* as well as the suffix *-dom*. The suffix *-hood* meant "condition" or "state of affairs"; it has no modern independent counterpart, however, and is unrelated to our word *hood* "covering for the head." The basic numerals in the classical languages, which were free forms in Greek and Latin just as the corresponding numerals are in English, have provided the bound roots out of which many English compounds are formed, e.g., *penta-* in *pentagon* "having five angles," *sept-* in *septet* "a group of seven," *oct-* in *octagonal* "having eight angles", *uni-* in *unilateral* "one sided."

The opposite development, whereby a bound morpheme escapes into the list of free morphemes, is unusual. This is even more true of affixes than it is of roots. There has been a recent trend in the language to detach affixes and elevate them to the status of roots. A typical example is *anti*. We can say things like, "It doesn't matter what the principle is, he is so stubborn that he's bound to be anti." There are even a few forms, originally affixes, that have been detached to become independent words themselves, e.g., the form *pro* from the word *professional*, which originally meant "one who declares (*fess*) forth (*pro-*)." We no longer think of *pro* in a phrase like *pro golfer* as having anything to do with the prefix *pro-* that occurs in *process, provide, profess*. Since the mid-eighties, the negative prefix *dis-* has been used as a verb meaning "insult, show disrespect, criticize," as in *dissed, dissing*. "The Lady is a Trans," meaning "a transgendered person," was a 1996 musical hit. The latter two examples are still considered "non-standard." Other examples of this kind, more or less acceptable, include *hyper, mini, maxi, stereo*. In any case, the status of these items is still influx and their occasional encroachment into the realm of free roots does not change the basic norm that affixes are bound forms which must be attached to stems.

Group-Work Activities

Try to find the affixes in the following words:

socialist	prosperity	democracy
civility	harmony	freedom
equality	justice	patriotism
dedication	integrity	friendship

1. How do you understand these words?

2. What are their socialist values?
3. How do you understand "rule of law"?

You can visit http://210.72.20.108/special/class3/search.jsp (中国重要政治词汇对外翻译标准化专题库) to find its translation in Chinese.

1. There is something called "a rule-of-law culture in guiding our thinking" (法治思维). Do you agree that the rule of law can guide our thinking?
2. How important is "the rule-of-law culture" for us to cope with the unprecedented challenges and move the reform further in the new era?

4.2.3 Allomorphs

The previous unit showed us that a **morpheme** is the smallest unit that pairs a consistent form with a consistent meaning. But when we say that the form of a morpheme is consistent, there's still some room for variability in the form. Think back to what you know about phonology and remember that a given phoneme can show up as different allophones depending on the surrounding environment. Morphemes work the same way: a given morpheme might have more than one **allomorph**. Allomorphs are forms that are related to each other but slightly different, depending on the surrounding environment. A simple example is the English word *a*. It means something like "one of something, but not any particular one", like in these examples: *a* book, *a* skirt, *a* friend, *a* phone call.

But if the word following *a* begins with a vowel instead of a consonant, then the word *a* changes its form: *an* apple, *an* ice cream cone, *an* iguana, *an* idea.

The two forms *a* and *an* are slightly different in their form, but they clearly both have the same meaning. And each one shows up in a different predictable environment: *a* before words that start with consonants and *an* before words that begin with vowels.

Another example of allomorphs in English is in the plural morpheme. In written English, the form of the plural morpheme is spelled *-s*, as in *carrots, books, hats, friends, apples, iguanas*.

But it's spelled *-es* in words like *churches, bushes, quizzes*.

And in fact, even in the cases where it's spelled -*s*, it's pronounced as [s] for words that end in a voiceless segment (*carrots, books, cliffs*) and as [z] for words that end in voiced sounds (*worms, dogs, birds*). So, it's got two written forms (-*s* and -*es*) and three spoken forms ([s], [z], [ɨz]), but with a consistent meaning of "more than one". Each form is an allomorph of the plural morpheme.

4.3 Morphological Processes: Inflection and Derivation

The distinction between grammatical and lexical morphemes is relevant with respect to two different types of morphological process: derivation and inflection. Derivation is one way of forming new words, whereas inflection distinguishes different grammatical forms of the same word. **Inflectional morphemes** (or inflectional suffixes) are thus bound grammatical morphemes, whereas **derivational morphemes** (or derivational affixes) are bound lexical morphemes.

The morpheme or combination of morphemes to which a derivational or inflectional morpheme is attached is called the **base**. For example, if we start with a verb that describes an action, like *teach* and we add the morpheme -*er*, we derive a morphologically complex noun, teacher, that refers to the person who does the action of teaching. That same -*er* morpheme does the same job in *singer, dancer, baker,* and *writer*.

While a base can consist of several morphemes, the term **root** is used for single morphemes that are not affixes such as *question* in *unquestionable* or *coast* and line in *coastlines*.

Most roots in English consist of free morphemes, but there is also a case to be made out for bound roots such as *rasp-* in *raspberry* and possibly *Corn-* in *Cornish*.

4.3.1 Derivational Morphology

The derivation is the process of creating a new word. The new, derived word is related to the original word, but it has some new components of meaning to it, and often it belongs to a new category. One of the most common ways that English derives new words is by affixing a derivational morpheme to a base.

Notice that each of the morphologically complex derived words is related in meaning to the base, but it has a new meaning of its own. English also derives new words by prefixing, and while adding a derivational prefix does lead to a new word with a new meaning, it often doesn't lead to a category change.

Morphology fulfils two main functions in English. Morphemes can be used to form new words: beauty + ful > beautiful; danger + ous > dangerous; or to inflect verbs and nouns: look, look + s, look + ing, look +ed.

The first category is known as derivational morphology and it involves prefixation: re + turn > return; un + true > untrue. Suffixation: man + ly > manly; wicked + ness > wickedness or affixation involving both prefixation and suffixation: un + speak + able > unspeakable; sub + conscious + ly > subconsciously.

Prefixes, occurring commonly, are *be-*, *de-*, *en-*, *ex-*, *hyper-*, pre-, *pro-*, re-, sub-, super- and *trans-*. Prefixes alter meaning but do not always change the function of the word to which they are prefixed:

be	witch (n.)	bewitch (v.)
de	limit (v.)	delimit (v.)
en	rich (adj.)	enrich (v.)
ex	terminate (v.)	exterminate (v.)
hyper	market (n.)	hypermarket (n.)

Suffixes, used frequently, always change the class of the word to which they are attached: beauty (*n.*) + ful > beautiful (*adj.*); determine (*v.*) + action > determination (*n.*).

So here, there are some rules.

(a) Words ending in the morphemes *-acy*, *-action*, *-er/-or*, *-ess*, *-ity*, *-ment*, *-ness* and *-ship* tend to be nouns, democracy, actor, bewilderment, adoration, mistress, weakness, painter, soleminity, horsemanship.

(b) Words ending in *-ise/ize* tend to be verbs: epitomize, hospitalise.

(c) Words ending in *-able, -ed, -ful, -ical, -ive, -less, -like, -ous,* and *-y* tend to be adjective: enjoyable, polished, comical, diminutive.

And words which end in "-ly" tend to be adverbs: He ran home *quickly*; She locked the doors *securely*.

Although the suffixes tend to be associated with particular word classes, it is always worth remembering that, in English, it is only safe to judge the class of an item when it has been seen in context. Thus, although *lovely* and *friendly* end in *-ly* they function as adjectives and not as adverbs: a lovely girl, a friendly welcome.

Most of the examples of affixes in English that we have discussed so far have been of **derivational affixes**; affixes that attach to other morphemes to form new words that are separate entries in our mental dictionary, or lexicon.

Derivational prefixes and suffixes both derive new words, but the attachment of derivational prefixes usually results in a word of the same category as the word to which the prefix attaches. So, *happy* and *unhappy* are both adjectives; the prefix *un-* doesn't change the category of *happy*. The attachment of derivational suffixes, on the other hand, usually does result in a change in the category of the word; the adjective *happy* becomes the noun *happiness* with the addition of the suffix *-ness*. But notice that even though prefixes don't change the category of a word, they do create words with different meanings. *Happy* and *unhappy* are each listed separately in our mental lexicon (and in the dictionary). Although prefixes in English do not change the category of a word (they do in many other languages), prefixes are nevertheless derivational affixes, changing the meaning of the words they attach to.

Like derivational suffixes, prefixes in English attach to words or roots of a particular category. For example, *ex-* attaches to nouns to derive nouns. *Ex-* cannot attach to verbs or adjectives:

ex + noun = noun   ex + verb = *   ex + adjective = *
ex-president *ex-mystify *ex-modern
ex-friend *ex-activate *ex-fixable
Here are a few more examples of prefixes in English and the words they

can attach to:

anti + noun = noun　　**de + verb = verb**　　**in + adjective = adjective**
anti-depressant　　de-activate　　in-eligible
anti-establishment　　de-nude　　in-competent

4.3.2 Inflectional Morphology

The last section talked about derivation, which is one of the jobs that morphology can do. The other big job that morphemes have is inflection.

English has what is sometimes called a "**poor**" or "**weak**" inflectional system. This means that English has relatively little inflectional morphology compared to languages that have morphologically "rich" systems, systems that morphologically express case, gender, number, tense, and other grammatical relationships in productive ways.

We've seen that we attach derivational affixes to words or roots to derive new words. Most derivational suffixes have the effect of changing the syntactic category, or part of speech of a word. For example, *-ity*, when added to an adjective such as *divine*, creates a noun, *divinity*. A different class of affixes, **inflectional affixes**, do not change the category of the word to which they attach, nor do they create new dictionary entries. Rather, these affixes express grammatical information—information about case, tense, aspect, number, person, and so on, without changing the meaning of the roots.

English has only eight inflectional affixes, as shown in Table 4.1. As you can see, only English nouns, verbs, adjectives, and adverbs—**all open classes of words**—take inflectional affixes. Closed classes of words, prepositions, conjunctions, quantifiers, etc., take no inflectional affixes in English.

Inflectional affixes always follow derivational ones if both occur in a word, which makes sense if we think of inflections as affixes on fully formed words. For example, the words *antidisestablishmentarianism* and *uncompartmentalize* each contain a number of derivational affixes, and the inflectional affixes must occur at the end, i. e. *antidisestablishmentarianisms* and *uncompartmentalized*.

We can also see from Table 4.1 that not only does English have few inflectional affixes but also that possessive, plural, and third-person singular are identical in form; they are all -*s*. The past participle affix -*ed* is also sometimes identical in form to the past tense affix -*ed*.

Table 4.1 Inflectional Affix –*s* in English

Nouns	Verbs	Adjectives
Possessive -*s* Lee's book	3rd person, singular -*s* Lee walks	comparative -*er* Lee is taller.
Plural -*s* six books	past tense -*ed* Lee walked	superlative -*est* Lee is tallest
	present participle -*ing* Lee is walking	
	past participle -*ed*/-*en* Lee has walked Lee has eaten	

We might think that the overlap in forms of inflectional affixes would cause confusion and make English harder to learn than languages with unambiguous inflectional endings. For example, children would confuse verbs with nouns because both can be affixed with -*s*, but this is not the case. Children appear to have no problem mastering the English inflectional system. They also acquire inflectional affixes and function words in a particular order. For example, psychologist Roger Brown demonstrated that English-speaking children acquire inflectional affixes in the same general order; for example, the present progressive (aux + -*ing*, as in *is running*) is acquired before possessive inflections (-*'s*, as in *the dog's ball*), which is acquired before regular third person forms (-*s*, as in *She runs fast*) and so on.

Also, children's acquisition of the plural inflection -*s* underscores the productivity of this affixation rule in English over other possible plural formation rules. Children typically overgeneralize -*s*, producing forms such as *gooses*, *deers*, and *childs*, before they master the adult irregular forms *geese*, *deer*, and *children*. The "regular" inflectional rule for plural in English thus appears to be -*s* affixation, and it is no wonder that new words in the language take this inflection in the plural rather than through a change in the vowel (*geese/mice*) by some affix other than -*s* (-*en* in *children* or -*i* in *foci*), or by nothing at all (*deer/elk*). For example, we send *faxes* (not *faxi*) and *e-mails* (not *e-mailen*), and we create *blogs* (not *blog*).

4.4 Compound Words

One very productive way that new words are derived in English is by compounding, that is, combining two free morphemes to create a new word. Endocentric compounds have a head that determines the meaning and the category of the compound, and in English, the head is the second part of the compound.

Compounding is different from affixation. In affixation, a bound morpheme is affixed to a base. Compounding derives a new word by joining two morphemes that would usually be free morphemes.

For example, if we take the free morpheme *green*, an adjective, and combine it with the free morpheme *house*, a noun, we get the new word *greenhouse*. We can tell that this is a new word because its meaning is different from what we would get if we just combined the two words to make a phrase. We could walk down the street describing houses: *This is a brown house and this one here is a tall house and here is a red house and here is a green house.* But a *greenhouse* is something different from a house that's green! It's a new word derived by compounding.

Another way that words derived by compounding differ from words derived by affixation is that a compound word doesn't really have a base or root that determines the meaning of the word. Instead, both pieces of a compound make a sizeable contribution to the meaning. For example, *yoga pants* are pants that you wear to do yoga, and *emerald green* is the particular colour of green that emeralds are. So, it doesn't make sense to say that compounds have a root.

On the other hand, there is one part of a compound that has a special role, which we can see if we think about the categories of the words that make up a compound.

Each compound is made up of a different category of the word on the left plus a verb on the right. But in each case, the compound word is a verb. Even if both parts of a compound contribute to the meaning of the compound, it's the head of a compound that determines its category. We say that English is a head-final language because in English the second part of the compound determines the category of the compound. Some languages are head-initial, with the head as the first element in a compound.

In many compounds, the head determines the category and also constrains the meaning of the compound. So, *dog food* is a kind of food, not a kind of dog, and *yoga pants* are a kind of pants, not a variety of yoga. Compounds like this, where the meaning relationship between the head and the whole compound is obvious, are called **endocentric**. But in some compounds, the meaning relationship is not so transparent. For example, *a redhead* is a person, not a kind of head; *a nest egg* is money that you've saved, not a kind of egg; *a workout* is not a particular kind of out, and *Facebook* is not a book at all! Compounds where the meaning of the head does not predict the meaning of the compound are said to be **exocentric**.

Learning and Research Resources

- *Morphology (Journal)*

https://www.springer.com/journal/11525

Morphology publishes articles on morphology proper, as well as articles on the interaction of morphology with phonology, syntax, and semantics, the acquisition and processing of morphological information, the nature of the mental lexicon, and morphological variation and change. Its main focus is on formal models of morphological knowledge, morphological typology (the range and limits of variation in natural languages), the position of morphology in the architecture of the human language faculty, and the evolution and change of language. In addition, the journal deals with the acquisition of morphological knowledge and its role in language processing.

- **Wordart**

https://wordart.com/

Word Art.com is an online word cloud art creator that enables you to create amazing and unique word cloud art with ease. Professional quality results can be achieved in no time at all, even for users with no prior knowledge of graphic design.

• 微词云

https://www.weiciyun.com/

The wordcloud (also called tag cloud) is a data visualization technique which highlights the important textual data points from a big text corpus. The approach used creates a meaningful visualization of text which could really help to understand high prominence of words that appear more frequently.

• Padlet

https://zh-cn.padlet.com/dashboard

Padlet is a place where you can create a single or multiple walls that are able to house all the posts you want to share. From videos and images to documents and audio, it is literally a blank slate. It's collaborative, too, allowing you to involve students, other teachers and even parents and guardians.

Summary

In this chapter, we see that many words are made up of meaningful pieces called morphemes. In English, the most common bound morphemes are suffixes and prefixes, which can be affixed to words to derive new words, or can convey grammatical information via inflection. Although English has a very productive system of derivational morphology, its inflectional morphology is quite sparse. We have used some indigenous languages to examine the kinds of grammatical information that can be represented with inflectional morphemes. We also have learned that compounding is a very productive means of deriving new words in English by combining two words. While most compounds are endocentric and have a head that determines the meaning and category of the word, for exocentric compounds, the meaning of the compound drifts over time, leaving the compound without a head.

> **Learning Highlights: Read and Think—Linguistics and Life**
>
> Let us review what are characteristics of morphology. In this chapter, we learned that words have multiple affixes and they can be divided into different morphological types of affixes. Most of the different affixation processes used in languages have yet to be systematically examined in the production domain. Also, in order to have a viable account of language production, we need to include all of the morphologically complex types of words used in languages. An examination of different morphologically systems may well lead us to different types of mental lexical representations and different production processes than these envisaged so far.
>
> 1. How do you understand that morphological processes are complex?
> 2. Do you know any other morphological system?
> 3. Do you agree that different morphologically systems may lead to different types of mental lexical representations?
> 4. How much do you know about the morphology of Putonghua?
>
> Here is a brief introduction to morphemes in Putonghua:
>
> *In Putonghua, morpheme can be divided into different classifications from various perspectives. From the view of number of syllables, it can be divided into monosyllabic morpheme and multi-syllabic morpheme. For the purpose of giving a clear idea of it for the students who attend to summer program in China, each classification will be explained in the following parts with typical examples.*
>
> *The monosyllabic morpheme is the morpheme composed of only one syllable, which is the basic form of the morpheme in Chinese language. It is a syllable when being read while a character when being written such as* 人 , 去 , 我 , 民 , 往 , 其 , 很 , 虽 , 自 , 以 , *etc. The monosyllabic morphemes in Chinese are very powerful because they all have strong ability of word formation.*

81

For the multi-syllabic morpheme, some of them are disyllabic morphemes. When being read, they are just one syllable, but two characters when being written, with only one meaning. There are mainly two types of disyllabic morphemes in Chinese language. The first group is the compound words, which will be further divided into two types. The first kind is the words which have the same initial consonants such as 秋千, 蜘蛛, 流连 *and* 犹豫. *The other type is the words with the similar simple or compound vowels like* 橄榄, 徜徉, 怂恿 *and* 肮脏, *to name but a few.*

*T*he *second category of the disyllabic morpheme is the loan words of transliteration like* 葡萄, 菩萨, 咖啡 *and* 马达. *For such kind of words, the students for online Chinese Lessons may feel easy to learn and understand. In addition, the morphemes with three or more syllables are mostly the loan words or words for places. The frequently used words of such type might be* 巧克力, 白兰地, 尼古丁, 木乃伊, 歇斯底里 *and* 可口可乐.

Usually speaking, the dissyllabic morphemes and multi-syllabic morphemes can form words independently. And some others can form words after combining with other morphemes. Of course, morpheme can be divided into more classifications except from the perspective of number of syllables. We can also divide them from the views of semantics and grammar into morphemes with different values.

1. How do you understand the potential of Chinese monosyllabic morphemes in word formation?

2. Is the word-building stem always regular?

3. How is the word-building system of Chinese different from that of English?

For all its symbolism about the freewheeling human spirit, though, irregularity is tightly encapsulated in the word-building system; the system as a whole is quite cuspy. Irregular forms are roots, which are found inside stems, some of which can be formed by regular inflection. This layering not only predicts many of the possible and also impossible words of English.

Turning to a syntactic hierarchy, we might want to observe that the smallest elements of syntax are morphemes. Whether these morphemes are either nonlexical (as in the plural inflections /s/ or /iz/—cats, houses) or

4 Morphology

lexical (= lexeme—cat, house), their function is to constitute words; words are gathered into syntactic phrases; phrases are gathered into sentences... and beyond the sentence, if we wish our hierarchical theory to account for reading as well as speaking and writing, we could include constituents such as the paragraph. But clearly, morpheme, word, phrase and sentence are again constituents of the syntactic grammar of English.

Research Fronts

Chloë R. Marshall and Heather K. J. van der Lely did a research about irregular past tense forms in English.

...The cognitive processes underlying inflectional morphology have been, and continue to be, hotly debated (for a review, see Pinker 1999). Much research has focused on the English past tense, for which verbs fall into two groups: those that take a regular suffix -ed (e.g. walked, jogged) and those that take an irregular form (e.g. ran, flew)...

They used data from children to see how children with specific language impairment contribute to models of morphology.

13 children with G-SLI participated in the study. They were selected on the basis of a persistent deficit in grammatical production and comprehension, as revealed by standardized language tests and by tests designed specifically to target the complex grammatical structures that this group find so difficult.

Their study shows that children with G-SLI (Grammatical Speicifific Language Impairment) produced fewer tense-marked irregulars than expected for their age, and fewer over regularizations than their language-matched controls.

...The study of irregular past tense morphology reported in this paper complements studies of regular past tense inflection in revealing the cumulative effects of deficits in syntax, morphology and phonology on the construction of morphologically complex forms (van der Lely 2005; Marshall and van der Lely 2006, 2007a). To gather these findings provides support for a model of

morphology where regular forms are created by a rule whereas irregular forms are stored in the lexicon, and where phonology has a significant impact on the actual form of the verb that is produced...

Self-Study Activities

1. What are TWO key differences between inflectional and derivational morphemes in English?

2. In the words below, identify all bound, free, derivational, and inflectional morphemes.

nonconformist   decontextualized   repeating   upon   scariest   untested   carelessly.

3. What type of grammatical information does the inflectional affix in the word speeches communicate?

A. Number   B. Tense   C. Subject agreement   D. Case

4. What type of grammatical information does the inflectional affix in the word *climbed* communicate?

A. Number   B. Tense   C. Subject agreement   D. Case

5. In the sentence, "The room contained a bearskin rug," what kind of compound is *bearskin*?

A. Endocentric   B. Exocentric

6. In the sentence, "Randy worked as a cowhand on the ranch," what kind of compound is *cowhand*?

A. Endocentric   B. Exocentric

7. Which of the following best describes the derivation of the word assignment?

A. Noun + -ment → Verb.
B. Adjective + -ment → Noun.
C. Verb + -ment → Noun.
D. Verb + -ment → Verb.

8. Which of the following best describes the derivation of the word skillful?

A. Adjective + -ful → Verb.
B. Adjective + -ful → Adjective.
C. Verb + -ful → Noun.
D. Noun + –ful → Adjective.

9. Can you try to make a padlet about a morphological topic? For example, you can make a padlet about inflectional morphemes.

10. Do you know the following words? Can you guess their meanings?

4 Morphology

How many morphemes in each of them? Can you find any characteristics of them?

孬 nao 嫑 biao 烎 yín 槑 mei 囧 jiǒng 兲 tiān 夻 nì 奱 jiao 嚻 jiao

Further Reading

P. H. Matthews' *Morphology* (2nd ed., Cambridge: Cambridge University Press, 1991) describes English morphology.

Laurie Bauer's *English word formation* (Cambridge, UK: Cambridge University Press, 1983) and P. H. Matthews' *Morphology: An introduction to the theory of word structure* (Cambridge, UK: Cambridge University Press, 1976) are worth of reading.

Outline

Ⅰ. The study of how morphemes come together to make words is called **morphology**. Morphology includes the study of the system of rules underlying our knowledge of the structure of words.

Ⅱ. A **morpheme** is the smallest abstract linguistic unit that serves to carry meaning (not the smallest unit of meaning). The most basic elements in a language are its sounds. The next level upward is morpheme.

Ⅲ. Morphemes work the same way: a given morpheme might have more than one **allomorph**. Allomorphs are forms that are related to each other but slightly different, depending on the surrounding environment.

Ⅳ. A morpheme that can occur by itself is a **free morpheme**; a morpheme that only occurs attached to another morpheme is a **bound morpheme**.

A. Bound morphemes are morphemes that cannot stand alone and must be attached to another morpheme or word. The process that one morpheme attaches to other morphemes or words is called affixation.

B. **Inflectional morphemes** (or inflectional suffixes) are thus bound grammatical morphemes, whereas **derivational morphemes** (or derivational affixes) are bound lexical morphemes.

Ⅴ. The derivation is the process of creating a new word. One of the most common ways that English derives new words is by affixing a derivational morpheme to a base.

VI. Inflectional affixes always follow derivational ones if both occur in a word, which makes sense if we think of inflections as affixes on fully formed words.

VII. One very productive way that new words are derived in English is by compounding, that is, combining two free morphemes to create a new word.

   A. Compounding is different from affixation. In affixation, a bound morpheme is affixed to a base. Compounding derives a new word by joining two morphemes that would each usually be free morphemes.

     i) Compounds can be **endocentric** if the meaning relationship between the head and the whole compound is obvious.

     ii) Compounds can be **exocentric** if the meaning of the head does not predict the meaning of the compound.

5 Syntax

5.1 Introduction

In this chapter, we will proceed to explore the next level of language structure, *syntax*. Sounds make up morpheme; morphemes make up words, and words come together in sentences; in linguistics, the study of how words come together in sentences is called syntax. This chapter is concerned with one facet of structure, English syntax: how words are grouped and ordered within sentences, clauses, and phrases. The crucial insight is that forming sentences is not a mere matter of placing words in order one at a time. Rather, just as the phonemic/phonetic distinction underlies the mere assemblage of sounds, and just as conglomerations of morphemes underlie the surface rendition of words, in syntax there is what lies beneath and what is on the surface.

5.1.1 Noam Chomsky

In 1957, the graduate student Noam Chomsky wrote a short book called *Syntactic Structures*. In so doing, he introduced generative grammar, now the most visible linguistic theory in the world. In *Syntactic Structures*, Chomsky outlined a theory of grammar based on questions about language that were very different from those asked by the scholars before him. Chomsky sought to explain what underlies the human ability to speak and understand language. He wondered what makes up a human language and whether we can construct theories about linguistic systems that can be scientifically tested.

One of Chomsky's foundational concepts was that syntax is a module of the generation of a sentence that is distinct from its meaning (i.e., its semantics). Earlier, it was generally thought that expressing meaning and syntax were more or less the same process. Chomsky called attention to facts such as *The dog bit the man* and *The man was bitten by the dog* have the same meaning but different syntax. Also, a sentence that is syntactically well-formed can be semantically meaningless. This sentence is termed grammatical albeit nonsensical. Chomsky proposed therefore that there is a mental level that generates grammatical sentences, with their meaning being a separate generative process.

Chomsky's basic idea was that this process is innate, and he called it *universal grammar*. One of Chomsky's crucial insights was that children do not make all the mistakes that we would expect them to.

Chomsky first inaugurated this idea in what was published in 1957 as *Syntactic Structures*. Within 10 years, this approach to syntax became the dominant one in linguistics, and it is taught universally today.

5.1.2 Generative Grammar

Chomsky's theory of grammar is called *generative* because it is designed to describe a precise and finite set of rules that generates (or has as its out-put) the possible sentences in a language. Mathematical operations such as division and multiplication are also generative; though many of you had to memorize multiplication tables in school, what you also learned was how to multiply, and the knowledge of that operation allows you (now) to multiply any numbers you want to. We can think of generative grammar in the same way; we don't memorize all the sentences in a language in order to speak it; rather, we learn or acquire a system of rules that allow us to produce and understand the possible sentences in the language. Chomsky proposed that some of these generative rules might also be grounded in Universal Grammar and thus be common to all languages. Chomsky's approach to language was an enormous departure from the thinking of the time, and this is why Chomsky's influence on the study of language is sometimes referred to as the "Chomskyan revolution." In his view, in order to answer the question: *what is a language*? It is necessary to study language from the inside out, as a system, rather than as a corpus, a list of words and sentences in the language. For Chomsky, the most interesting question to ask about language was, "What is it that we know about language in order to speak it and understand it?" Andrew Camie gives a definition of generative grammar in his book *Syntax: A Generative Introduction*.

5 Syntax

The underlying thesis of generative grammar is that sentences are generated by a subconscious set of procedures (like computer programs). These procedures are part of our minds (or our cognitive abilities if you prefer). The goal of syntactic theory is to model these procedures. In other words, we are trying to figure out what we subconsciously know the syntax of our language. In generative grammar, the means for modelling these procedures is through a set of formal grammatical rules.

When we describe the syntax of a given language, we want to define a set of rules that, when followed, is capable of generating all grammatically acceptable sentences in that language. This set of rules should not produce any ungrammatical sentences.

For example, if we are going to posit a set of rules for the English language, we should be able to follow those rules to produce a phrase like "An angry dog bit a man." Following these same rules should prevent us from creating a sentence like "A dog angry a man bit."

Learning and Research Resources

• Taylor & Francis Online
https://www.tandfonline.com/

Taylor & Francis is an international academic publisher with offices worldwide. It publishes more than 2,100 journals, over 4,000 new books each year. You could find any topic you are interested in at this site. Please find some latest research about Generative Grammar at Tayloronline.com.

5.2 Basic Syntactic Notions

5.2.1 Constituents

As we mentioned in the first chapter, linguists do not care about the grammatical rules or what you have learned in your grammar book; however, it does not mean there is no rule. At the centre of any discussion of syntax is the notion of **constituency**: the idea that syntactic units are not simply arbitrarily grouped and ordered but form identifiable units. **Constituent** is a word or a group of words that functions as a single unit. Traditionally, syntacticians have identified four different levels of structure at which constituents can occur

sentences (largest) → **clauses** → **phrases** → **words (smallest)**

The largest constituent is the sentence; the smallest is the word. Between these two extremes are clauses and phrases, though as they will be demonstrated later, sometimes sentences and clauses are identical: a declarative sentence, for instance, may consist of one main clause. There are two different types of constituents: immediate constituents and ultimate constituents. Exactly which elements constitute immediate constituents depends upon what level of structure (sentence, clause, phrase) is being considered. To illustrate this point, consider the sentence below:

Robbin Mayfield and his graffiti-removal crew drive an old Wonderbread truck.

At the highest level, the sentence itself is a constituent. But within the sentence, one can find several immediate constituents: separate units into which a given structure can be divided. For instance, the sentence can be divided into two immediate constituents: the **subject** (*Robbin Mayfield and his graffiti-removal crew*) and the **predicate** (*drive an old Wonderbread truck*). The predicate, in turn, contains two additional immediate constituents: the verb (*drive*) and the noun phrase (*an old Wonderbread truck*). At the level of the word, the lowest level of structure, we find the ultimate constituents: the individual words themselves (*Robbin, Mayfield, and, his, etc.*). The details of exactly how notions such as subject and verb are defined will be described in greater detail in subsequent sections of the chapter. At this stage, however, it is reasonable to consider why *an old Wonderbread truck* is considered a constituent, but *his graffiti-removal crew drive an* is not.

5.2.2 Linear and Hierarchical Structuring of Constituents

English has constraints on both the linear ordering of constituents and on their hierarchical groupings. As an illustration of the difference between the **linear** and **hierarchical** nature of syntax, consider the expression *foreign* *language specialist*, which exemplifies the notion of structural ambiguity: two different meanings depending upon how the words in the expression are grouped.

How *foreign language specialist* is interpreted depends not just on how the words are ordered but upon whether *language* is grouped with *foreign* or *specialist*, as schematized in (a) and (b) below:

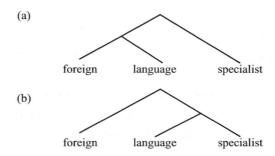

In (a), because foreign and language are grouped, the phrase has the meaning of "a specialist in foreign languages." In (b), in contrast, the grouping of language and specialist creates the meaning of "a language specialist who is foreign-born."

Groupings of this nature constitute the core of English syntax, and along with constraints on the linear order of constituents, they allow linguists to describe the form and function of various kinds of constructions in English, from the sentence down to the word.

5.2.3 Form and Function

Constituents can be described in terms of their form and their function. In the clause *The child is healthy*, healthy has the form of an adjective phrase and the function of a subject complement. The form of some constituents can be determined by the particular suffixes that they contain as well as their positions relative to other constituents. *Healthy* contains an ending *-y* which is used to convert nouns to adjectives. Thus, *healthy* is derived from *health*, *tasty* from *taste*, *wealthy* from *wealth*, and so forth. *Healthy* is also a predicative rather than an attributive adjective: it occurs following the linking verb *is* rather than directly before the noun, as in the *healthy child*. *Healthy* is functioning in the clause as a subject complement because it follows the linking verb *is* and describes the subject of the sentence, *the child*. The kinds of criteria applied above to identify adjectives and subject complements can be applied to all forms and functions in English. Such an analysis reveals that constituents have forms at all four levels of structure:

Word Classes: noun, verb, adjective, adverb, preposition, etc.
Phrases: noun phrase, verb phrase, adjective phrase, adverb phrase, prepositional phrase
Clauses: main clause, dependent clause
Sentences: declarative, interrogative, imperative, exclamatory

While all types of phrases, clauses, and sentences are given in the list above, only a sampling of word classes is given, since additional classes exist in English (e.g. articles, pronouns, conjunctions).

English has far fewer functions, and these functions are restricted to elements occurring within clauses (both main and subordinate). Thus, the functions below are often referred to as clause functions:

Subject
Predicator
Complement (subject and object)
Object (direct and indirect)
Adverbial

Since constituent forms and functions are key components of syntax, the next two sections provide an overview of some of the important form classes in English and the particular clause functions that these particular forms can have.

5.3 Word Classes

In this section, we start observing how words behave so that we can group them into categories. Syntactic categories, which you might think of as "parts of speech", are group words that behave similarly into similar categories. Once we've figured out what category a word belongs to, we can predict how it will interact with other words from other categories, for example in compound words.

One established model of word class categorisation is that of the Comprehensive Grammar of the English Language by Quirk, Greenbaum, Leech and Svartvik (1985) (CGEL's word classes), where the following word classes—or parts of speech—are distinguished:

I	NOUN	*John, room, answer, play*
II	ADJECTIVE	*happy, steady, new, large, round*
III	FULL VERB	*search, grow, play*
IV	ADVERB	*steadily, completely, really*
V	PREPOSITION	*of, at, in, without, in spite of*
VI	PRONOUN	*he, they, anybody, one, which*
VII	DETERMINER	*the, a, that, every, some*
VIII	CONJUNCTION	*and, that, when, although*
IX	MODAL VERB	*can, must, will, would*
X	PRIMARY VERB	*be, have, do*
XI	NUMERAL	*one, two, three; first, second, third*
XII	INTERJECTION	*oh, ah, ugh, phew*
Words of unique function		*not (negative particle), to (infinitive marker)*

The first four of these word classes—nouns, full verbs, adjectives and adverbs—are often referred to as **open classes** because the number of words they comprise is not restricted and new members can constantly be added. The number of prepositions, pronouns, determiners, conjunctions, modal and primary verbs, however, is limited and not easily subject to change. These word classes are thus called **closed classes**.

Learning and Research Resources

- *Cambridge Dictionary*

https://dictionary.cambridge.org/zhs/

Cambridge Dictionary is a free dictionary for helping you find the categories of words.

Group-Work Activities

两岸猿声啼不住,轻舟已过万重山。

"the monkeys who screamed from,
the two sides without stopping."

"On two sides apes call, not stopping;
this little boat has passed ten thousand layered mountains."

"The screams of monkeys on either bank
Had scarcely ceased echoing in my ear
When my skiff had left behind it."

1. Which version of the translation is more accessible?
2. Can you find the predicate verbs in these three versions?
3. How do you like these three versions? Which one do you prefer? Why?

Appreciate more poems as follows and analyse the constitutes of syntax.

(1) 折戟沉沙铁未销,自将磨洗认前朝。

We dig out broken halberds buried in the sand,
And wash and rub these relics of an ancient war.

东风不与周郎便,铜雀春深锁二乔。

Had the east wind refused to give a helping hand,
Southern beauties would have been captives on northern shore.

(2) **Snow Adopted After the Tune of Chin Yuan Chun**
   沁园春·雪
   North country scene:
   北国风光,
   A hundred leagues locked in ice,

千里冰封,
A thousand leagues of whirling snow.
万里雪飘。
Both sides of the Great Wall
望长城内外,
One single white immensity.
惟余莽莽;
The Yellow River's swift current
大河上下,
Is stilled from end to end.
顿失滔滔。
The mountains dance like silver snakes
山舞银蛇,
And the highlands charge like wax-hued elephants,
原驰蜡象,
Vying with heaven in stature.
欲与天公试比高。
On a fine day, the land,
须晴日,
Clad in white, adorned in red,
看红装素裹,
Grows more enchanting.
分外妖娆。

This land so rich in beauty
江山如此多娇,
Has made countless heroes bow in homage.
引无数英雄竞折腰。
But alas! Chin Shih-huang and Han Wu-ti
惜秦皇汉武,
Were lacking in literary grace,
略输文采;
And Tang Tai-tsung and Sung Tai-tsu
唐宗宋祖,
Had little poetry in their souls;

> 稍逊风骚。
> *And Genghis Khan, Proud Son of Heaven for a day,*
> 一代天骄，成吉思汗，
> *Knew only shooting eagles, bow outstretched*
> 只识弯弓射大雕。
> *All are past and gone!*
> 俱往矣，
> *For truly great men*
> 数风流人物，
> *Look to this age alone.*
> 还看今朝。

5.3.1 Open Class Categories: Nouns, Verbs, Adjectives and Adverbs

Nouns

You've probably learned that nouns are words that describe a person, place or thing. But when we're studying morphology and syntax, we categorize words according to their behaviour, not according to their meaning. There are two elements to a word's behaviour:

What inflectional morphemes does the word take?

What is the word's syntactic distribution? In other words, what position does it occupy in a sentence?

What behaviour can we observe that allows us to categorise words as nouns? Looking at the inflectional morphology, we observe that most nouns in English have a singular and a plural form.

English uses a plural morpheme on a noun to indicate that there is more than one of something. But there is a subcategory of nouns that don't have plural forms. Mass nouns like *rice, water, money, oxygen* refer to things that aren't really countable, so the nouns don't get pluralized. Nouns that refer to abstract things (such as *justice, beauty, happiness*) behave like mass nouns too. If they don't have plural forms, why do we group them into the larger category of nouns? It's because their syntactic distribution behaves like that of count nouns. Most English nouns, singular, plural, or mass, can appear in a phrase following the word *the*.

In their syntactic distribution, **pronouns** (*I, me, you, we, us, they, them, he, him, she, her, it*) do the job that noun phrases do. A pronoun rarely appears with the, but it can replace an entire noun phrase. For example,

The woman read the book.
*The she read the book.
She *read* ***it.***

Verbs

Verbs behave differently to nouns. Morphologically, verbs have a past tense form and a progressive form. For a few verbs, the past tense form is spelled or pronounced the same as the bare form.

bare form	**past tense form**	**progressive form**
sing	sang	singing
think	thought	thinking
stay	stayed	staying

Adjectives

Adjectives appear in a couple of predictable positions. One is between the word *the* and a noun: *the red car; the clever students; the unusual song; the delicious meal.*

The other is following any of the forms of the verb *be*: *That car is red; The students are clever; The meal was delicious;* Many adjectives can be intensified with the words *very* or *more*: *very clever; more unusual; very delicious.*

And some adjectives (but not all) have comparative and superlative forms: *big – bigger – biggest; smart – smarter – smartest.*

The behaviour of adverbs is a little more difficult to observe. Unlike adjectives, adverbs don't have comparative or superlative forms, but like adjectives, they can be intensified with very or more: *very quickly; very cleverly; more importantly.*

The above examples illustrate that many adverbs are derived by affixing *-ly* to an adjective, but there are also many adverbs that are not derived this way, and there are also some common English words that have the *-ly* affix that aren't adverbs but adjectives, like *friendly, lonely, lovely*, so the affix is not a reliable clue. The syntactic distribution of adverbs is also a little slippery. Adverbs can precede or follow verbs (or verb phrases) to provide information about the verb: *The children sang beautifully; The students complained loudly about the pop quiz; They had just arrived when the fire alarm rang.*

And adverbs can precede adjectives or other adverbs to provide information about the adjective/adverb: *This meal is surprisingly tasty; An extremely expensive car drove by; The children finished their homework remarkably quickly.*

Because their behaviour is more variable than that of words in the other open-class categories, adverbs can be a challenge to identify.

The three syntactic categories of nouns, verbs and adjectives, are called open-class categories. The categories are considered open because when new words get added to the language, they are almost always in one of these three categories—the categories are open to new members. These categories are sometimes also called lexical categories or content words because these categories are the ones that do most of the lexical semantic work in a sentence: they convey most of the meaning of a sentence. The semantic content of the words from other categories (like *the, of, in, that*, etc.) is not as obvious as the semantics of the words from lexical categories.

Adverbs

You may have learned that adverbs modify verbs and that most end in *-ly*, such as *quickly, happily, enormously*, and so on. Many adverbs do not end in *-ly*, however, and not all adverbs modify only verbs. (And some adjectives end in *–ly* too: *friendly, lovely, manly.*)

Here is a short list of adverbs, including many that do not end in *-ly*.

still, never, often, fast, usually, just, perhaps, even, fortunately, once, twice, also, forcibly, sometimes

Certain adverb phrases (AdvP), like adjective phrases, can be modified by degree words (Deg). "Manner" adverbs (which can be paraphrased as "in X manner") can be modified in this way, as the following examples show: *very dejectedly, so slowly, awfully happily.*

Other adverbs can't be modified by degree words. (As you can see with *awfully*, some degree words are actually degree *adverbs* themselves!)

*very *once*
*so *sometimes*
*awfully *yet*

Unlike adjective phrases, which modify nouns, adverb phrases modify verbs and even entire clauses. They also differ from adjective phrases in that they contribute information about time, manner, reason, place, or cause (among other things).

5.3.2 Closed Class Categories: Function Words

There are also several smaller categories of words called **closed-class categories** because the language does not usually add new words to these categories. These categories don't have many members, maybe only a few dozen, in contrast with the many thousands of words in the open-class categories. They're the **function words** or **non-lexical categories** that do a lot of grammatical work in a sentence but don't necessarily have obvious semantic content.

Determiners

The category of **determiners** doesn't have many members but its members occur very frequently in English. The two little words *the* and *a* are the most recognizable members. Determiners most often appear before a noun.

Any word that can appear in the same position as the counts as a determiner, like demonstratives: *those* students, *these* oranges, *that* snake, *this* idea…Quantifiers and numerals also behave like determiners: *many* students, *twelve* students…And the words that you might have encountered as "possessive adjectives" or "possessive pronouns" behave like determiners as well: *my* sister, *your* idea, *their* car…

Prepositions

The category of **prepositions** seems to have slightly more obvious semantic content than most other closed classes. Prepositions often represent relationships in space and time. They also have consistent syntactic distribution, usually appearing with a noun phrase immediately following them: *on* the table, *in* the basket, *around* the block...

Conjunctions

A very small category of words that does an important job are the **conjunctions**. There are only three conjunctions, *and, or, but*. The job that conjunctions do is to conjoin two words or phrases that belong to the same category: oranges *and* lemons, strong *or* fast...

Complementisers

You might have learned that words like *because* and *although* are a type of conjunction, but they don't behave like *and*, or, *but*. Their behaviour is more similar to a category of words we label as **complementisers**. Complementisers are function words that introduce a clause, which is a sentence embedded inside a larger sentence: Sam told us *that* she loved baseball; She hoped *that* the Blue Jays would win the World Series.

5.3.3 Auxiliaries

Auxiliaries are what you might have called "helping verbs" when you first learned about grammar: they help a lexical verb by providing grammatical information about a verb's tense or aspect, or other subtle elements of meaning. There are nine **modal auxiliaries**, which never change their form because they are never inflected: Kieran *can* sing really well; We *shall* decide by drawing straws.

The verbs *have, be*, and *do* sometimes behave like auxiliaries and sometimes like ordinary lexical verbs. Unlike the modal auxiliaries, *have, be* and *do* get inflected (*had, has, having, am, is, are, was, were, been, being, did, done, doing*), so even when they are auxiliaries, they are **non-modal**. Their inflection is not a clue to whether they are auxiliaries or not, so we have to look at their behaviour in the context of a sentence.

If a sentence includes a lexical verb or main verb, then *have, be* or *do* in that sentence is likely to be an auxiliary, helping the lexical verb. In the following examples, the lexical verbs (also known as main verbs) are bolded: Arlene is **writing** a novel; Beulah has **arrived** in Saskatoon; Carmen is **planning** her vacation.

In addition to their auxiliary functions, *have, be* and *do* also have some lexical meaning of their own. If there's no other verb in the clause, then *have*, *be*, or *do* is probably the main verb of a clause. In these examples the lexical verbs are bolded: Foster *is* proud of his sister; Green vegetables *are* important for good health.

If *have, be or do* serves as the lexical verb, then it might also have some auxiliaries helping out: Foster has *been* proud of his sister; Green vegetables might *be* important for good health.

Notice that not every sentence has an auxiliary, but every sentence does have a lexical verb.

5.4 Phrase

5.4.1 Types of Phrase

There are five commonly occurring types of phrase in English: noun phrases, adjective phrases, verb phrases, adverb phrases and prepositional phrases in simple sentences, as underlined in the following sentences:

(a) A **noun phrase** is a group of words with a noun as its head word. There can be up to three phrases in a simple sentence:

      1   2   3
The young man threw the old dog a bone.
      1   2   3
That rich man will build his eldest daughter a fine house.

(b) An **adjective phrase** is a group of words which modifies a noun. Like adjectives, these words can be either attributive (that is, usually preceding but occasionally following a noun):

The child, laughing happily, ran out of the house.
That utterly fascinating novel has been banned.

or predicative (this is, following a verb):

The letter was unbelievably rude.

He seemed <u>extremely pleasant.</u>

(c) A **verb phrase** is a group of words with a verb as headword. Verb phrases can be either finite:

He <u>has been singing</u>.

or non-finite:

<u>to have sung</u>

A simple sentence can have only one finite verb phrase:

He <u>may be following</u> us.

But a complex sentence may have several finite verb phrases:

When he <u>was invited</u> to give a lecture, he <u>was told</u> that all reasonable expenses <u>would be refunded</u>.

(d) An **adverb phrase** is a group of words which functions like an adverb; it often plays the role of telling us when, where, why or how an event occurred:

We are expecting him to come <u>next year</u>.
He <u>almost always</u> arrives on time.
He ran <u>very quickly</u>.

(e) A **preposition phrase** is a group pf words that begins with a preposition:

He arrived <u>by plane</u>.
Do you know that man <u>with the scar</u>?
We are <u>on very good terms</u>.

5.4.2 Head and Modifier

A phrase is characterised by the fact that it can take a particular slot in the structure of a sentence. Most types of phrases, the so-called endocentric phrases, can be realized by a single word, which on its own can fulfil the same syntactic function in a sentence:

Painters

Many painters | *felt attracted to the place*

The painters who moved to France after the war

A word which can stand for a phrase on its own is called its **head**, endocentric phrases are also called **headed phrases**. Such headed phrases can contain a number of other elements, which are structurally dependent on the head, and which are known as **modifiers**.

For instance, in noun phrases, the head of a noun phrase is a noun or a pronoun. It can be modified by adjective phrases, prepositional phrases, relative clauses, adverb phrases, etc. Apart from modifiers, noun phrases can also contain determiners. Although there is a certain overlap between modification and determination, the typical function of modifiers is to further describe what is expressed by the head, whereas the sole function of determiners is to establish reference, i.e. to identify the elements in the real world to which the phrase can be applied. Thus, in the case of a phrase such as *this fascinating book on linguistics*, the function of *this* can be seen as pointing out or identifying which of all the possible books is referred to in a particular context; *this* thus fulfils a determinative function, whereas *fascinating* and *on linguistics* describe *the book* more closely and are thus classified as modifiers.

Phrase structure rules have an important property, namely that of **recursion**. This is the property of having an instance of a phrasal form class as a constituent within the same form class; in other words, it is the ability to embed a form class within a form class of the same type.

The pieces of the bigger sentence are held together in order as a set of branches growing out of a common node. That node holds together each either with its or, each if with its then, as in the following diagram (the triangles are abbreviations for lots of underbrush that would only entangle us if shown in full):

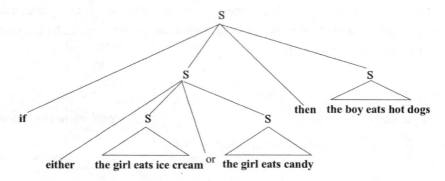

There is another reason to believe that a sentence is held together by a mental tree. So far we have been talking about stringing words into a grammatical order, ignoring what they mean. But grouping words into phrases is also necessary to connect grammatical sentences with their proper meanings, chunks of mentalese. We know that the sentence shown above is about a girl, not a boy, eating ice cream, and a boy, not a girl, eating hot dogs, and we know that the boy's snack is contingent on the girl's, not vice versa. That is because *girl* and *ice cream* are connected inside their own phrase, as are *boy* and *hot dogs,* as are the two sentences involving the girl. With a chaining device it's just one damn word after another, but with a phrase structure grammar the connectedness of words in the tree reflects the relatedness of ideas in mentalese. Phrase structure, then, is one solution to the engineering problem of taking an interconnected web of thoughts in the mind and encoding them as a string of words that must be uttered, one at a time, by the mouth.

5.4.3 Role of Phrase

While categories such as sentence or word also play an important role in general and non-academic discussions of language, the phrase does not. Nevertheless, the phrase is to be seen as a central unit of linguistic description. In particular, it must be borne in mind that it is through noun phrases—and not through nouns as words—that speakers can refer to concrete people or objects of the real world.

There is also psycholinguistic evidence to suggest that phrases are an important unit of language perception. For instance, experiments were carried out in which people were asked to listen to recorded sentences, into which distorting signals called clicks were inserted. The test subjects were then asked to locate the clicks in the sentence. Interestingly, subjects were able to identify the location of all clicks at phrase boundaries correctly, while there was a tendency to move the location of clicks within a phrase towards a phrase boundary.

> **Learning and Research Resources**
>
> ● **Academic Phrasesbank**
> http://www.phrasebank.manchester.ac.uk/
> **The Academic Phrasebank** is a general resource for academic writers. It aims to provide you with examples of some of the phraseological "nuts and bolts" of writing organised according to the main sections of a research paper or dissertation. Other phrases are listed under the more general communicative functions of academic writing. The phrases, and the headings under which they are listed, can be used simply to assist you in thinking about the content and organisation of your own writing, or the phrases can be incorporated into your writing where this is appropriate.
>
> ● **Write and Improve**
> https://writeandimprove.com/
> **Write & Improve** is a free tool for learners of English that marks writing in seconds. It is provided in association with Cambridge English (part of the University of Cambridge). You can use it to (a) practise writing English; (b) get your grade in seconds; (c) look at the feedback and make changes; 4) keep improving.

5.5 Clause

A sentence can consist of one or more clauses, a clause one or more phrases, a phrase one or more words, and a word one or more morphemes. The clause is a much more clearly definable unit of linguistic analysis than the sentence. A clause can occur as a **dependent (or subordinate) clause** or an **independent clause.**

In each complex sentence, we have at least two clauses: a main clause (that is most like a simple sentence) and at least one subordinate or dependent clause.

In the following examples, the main clause is italicised:

He believed that the earth was round.
He arrived as the clock was striking.

Noun clause

A **noun clause** is a group of words containing a finite verb and functioning like a noun:

He said *that he was tired.*

What you said was not true.

Noun clauses can often be replaced by pronouns: He said *this*.

When you are in doubt about how a clause functions in a sentence, you should see what can be substituted for it. All the following possibilities are acceptable:

I shall always remember (*John/him/his kindness/what John has done.*)

Thus, pronouns, nouns and noun phrases can usually be substituted for noun clauses.

Adjective clause

An adjective clause is often called a "relative clause" because it usually relates back to a noun whose meaning it modifies:

The dog *which won the competition* is an Alsatian.
The man *who taught my brother French* is now the headmaster.

When an adjective/relative clause begins with "that/which/whom" and is followed by a subject, the subordinator can be omitted:

The book *(that) John bought* is missing.
The coat *(which) she wrote is* red.

There is virtually no difference in meaning between:

The book which I bought...

or:

The book that I bought...

Although the third is the least formal and so the most likely to occur in spontaneous speech.

Occasionally an adjective clause can begin with "when": "I remember the day when we won the cup." or "where": "The town where they met was called Scarborough."

It is usually easy to decide whether a "when/where" clause is adjectival clauses.

Adverbial clause

An **adverbial clause** functions like an adverb in providing information about when, where, why, how or if for an action that occurs:

When he arrived, we were all sleeping.
Put it *where we can see it.*

Adverbial clauses are perhaps the most frequently used clauses in the language and, like adverbs, they are often mobile:

When he arrived, we were all sleeping.
We were all sleeping *when he arrived.*

A number of modern linguists use the term "clause" somewhat differently from the above classification. They call units containing a finite verb "finite clauses" and units containing non-finite verb forms such as "to see", "seeing" and "seen", "non-finite" clauses. A few examples will illustrate their usage. In the following sentences:

He went to Paris *because he wanted a rest*.
He went to Paris *to have a rest*.

Both italicised units tell us why he went to Paris but only the first one contains a finite verb.

When he heard the results he went home.
On hearing the results he went home.

The italicised units in the two sentences above function in similar ways, being distinguished mainly by the fact that the first examples contain finite verbs while the second examples non-finite verbs. Linguists who concentrate on the formal distinction, that is, the occurrence or non-occurrence of a finite verb in a unit, classify such units as clauses and phrases respectively. Those who concentrate on the functional similarities label both units as clauses, only distinguishing whether the verb is used as finite or non-finite. All linguists will agree that the italicised units in the following sentences function as subjects:

His behaviour is understandable.
To behave in this way is understandable.

But they will classify these subjects according to their preferred model. What is important is to be consistent in one's use of terminology.

5.6 Sentence

Sentences can exist independently, do not rely on any other unit and can be interpreted without reference to any other piece of language. Each sentence is an independent linguistics form, not included by virtue of any grammatical construction in any larger linguistic form.

An even simpler categorisation of "sentence" can be applied to the written medium in that we can define a sentence as "that linguistic unit which begins with a capital letter and ends with a full stop". Both definitions of "sentence" are useful but it will be worth studying further the types of sentences that occur in English and their internal construction. Sentences can be divided into four sub-types:

(a) **Simple sentences** contain only one finite verb:

Water <u>boils</u> at 100 Centigrade.
You <u>must</u> not say such things.

The finite verb may be composed of up to four auxiliaries plus a head verb:

He <u>was</u> never <u>seen</u> again.
We <u>can</u> hardly <u>ask</u> them for any more.

The term "simple" refers to the fact that the sentence contains only one finite verb. It does not imply that the sentence is easy to understand. The following sentence, for example, is simple in structure but semantically it is quite difficult:

Quangos are quasi-autonomous, non-governmental organisations.

(b) **Compound sentences** consist of two or more simple sentences linked by the co-ordinating conjunctions *and, but, so, either… or, neither … nor, or, then* and *yet*:

He ran out and (he) fell over the suitcase.
She arrived at nine, went up to her room and did not come down until noon.

In compound sentence, the shared elements in the conjoined simple sentences can be elided:

You may go in and (you may) talk to him for five minutes.

(c) Complex sentences consist of one simple sentence and one or more subordinate (or dependent) clauses. In "She became queen when her father died because she was the eldest child" we have one main clause: "She became queen" and two subordinate clauses: "when her father died" and "because she was the eldest child."

You will notice that each clause has a finite verb, "became", "died" and "was" in the example above, and that each subordinate clause begins with a subordinating conjunction. The commonest subordinating conjunctions in English are:

after: *She washed the dishes after she had cooked the meal.*
although/though: *Although they were poor, they were honest.*
as: *As John says, it's time to go.*
as…(as): *He is as tall as his father was.*
because: *He left the town because he did not like crowds.*
before: *He arrived before we did.*
if: *If you try hard you will certainly succeed.*
since: *I have not seen him since we left grammar school.*
until/till: *He worried about everything until his daughter arrived.*
when: *Time passes quickly when you are happy.*
where: *He built his home where his ancestors had lived.*
whether…or not: *John is the best runner whether he knows it or not.*
which/that: *This is the house which/that Jack built.*
while: *Do not cross the tracks while the lights are red.*

(d) Compound-complex sentences are, as their name suggests, a combination of complex sentences joined by co-ordinating conjunctions, for example, "I saw him when he arrived the first time but I didn't see him when he came again."

We have looked at the types of sentences that can occur and will now focus on the internal structure of a sentence. The basic pattern of the simple English sentence is (Adjunct)(Subject) Predicate (Object) (Complement) (Adjunct) usually given as (A) (S) P (O) (C) (A).

Where only the predicate is essential and the adjunct mobile ("A few simple examples will show how the formula works.") they can be divided into two parts: a noun part and a verb part. For example,

<u>The man</u>   <u>disappeared.</u>
noun part   verb part
<u>The poor young woman</u> <u>died</u>.
        noun part   verb part

We call the noun part a "subject" and the verb part a "predicate". We know that the subject is a unit because we can substitute "he" for "the man" and "she" for "the poor young woman". The verb part can usually be retrieved by asking such questions as "what did he do?/ what has he done?" and omitting the pronoun in answer. Notice that if our first sentence had been: *The man has disappeared.* Our question would retrieve the whole predicate, in this case "has disappeared". In the sentences: The man disappeared *yesterday. Quite suddenly* the man disappeared.

The italicised segment is called "adjuncts" because they can usually be deleted without causing grammatical loss. (Their removal would, of course, result in loss of information.) These adjuncts are usually quite mobile:

Suddenly the man disappeared.
The man *suddenly* disappeared.

If we take a different type of sentence, e. g. "John won't eat his breakfast." we see that it splits up into three parts: the subject "John", the predicate "won't eat" and the object "his breakfast". The object resembles the subject in that it is noun-like, but there are three main differences:

(a) The subject normally precedes the predicate. The object normally follows the predicate.

(b) The subject can usually be retrieved by putting who or what before the predicate, "Who won't eat his breakfast?" produces the answer "John", the subject. The object can be retrieved by putting "whom" or "what" after the predicate. "John won't eat what?" produces the answer "his breakfast", the object.

(c) When subject and objects are replaced by pronouns, there is often a different pronoun for the two positions:

John hit Peter. He hit him.
Mary hit Betty. She hit her.
John and Mary hit Peter and Betty. They hit them.

Adjuncts can occur in most sentences, e. g. *"Usually John won't eat his breakfast"* and *"John won't eat his breakfast usually."*

Looking now at such sentences as *"John is a fine teacher"* and *"Mary is becoming an excellent athlete"* we see that we again have three parts, but there is a fundamental difference between these sentences and sentences of the type Subject Predicate Object in that "John" = "a fine teacher" and "Mary" = "an excellent athlete". Such sentences always involve such verbs as BE, BECOME, SEEM and APPEAR, and GROW when they are used in such construction as *"He appeared the best choice" and "He grew weary."*

These verbs take complements and the complements can be a noun phrase and an adjective, a preposition + a noun phrase, or occasionally an adverb. The complements above are called "subject complements" because they provide information on the subjects. We can also have "object complements" as in *"They elected John President" and "John called his son Peter."*

Again, you will notice that the object "John" is the same as "President" and "his son" as "Peter". Sentences involving complements can also have adjuncts: *"John was a candidate yesterday" and "They elected John President yesterday."*

We can summarise the above data with examples as follows:

P *Go*
PA *Go quietly*
SP *John slept*
SPA *John slept quietly*
PO *Eat your breakfast*
SPO *John ate his breakfast.*
SPOA *John ate his breakfast quickly.*
SPC *John is a fool*
ASPC *At times John is a fool.*
SPOC *John called his brother a fool.*
SAPOC *John often called his brother a fool.*

In our examination of sentence patterns, four operations will prove useful. They are **insertion**, **deletion**, **substitution** and **transposition** (also called **permutation**). We can illustrate these operations as follows:

Insertion: This would involve changing such sentence as *"The child is clever"* into *"The little child is exceptionally clever."*

Deletion: In the sentence *"The tall man saw him last Friday"* we can delete the adjective "tall" and the adjunct "last Friday" leaving the grammatically acceptable: *"The man saw him."*

Substitution: In such sentences as *"The young man visited his mother"* we can substitute pronouns for both subject and object: *"He visited her."*

Often too, auxiliary verbs can replace verb phrases: *"He might have come, mightn't he?"* where "mightn't he" substitutes for "might he not have come".

Transposition: This involves the mobility of sentence constituents and we have already see how adjuncts can be transposed/moved from one part of a sentence to another. Other sentence constituents are less mobile, but occasionally, for effect, an object may precede both subject and predicate: *"Three men I saw."* However, such a sentence is much less usual than *"I saw three men."*

Learning and Research Resources

• Sentence Structure and Types of Sentences

https://academicguides.waldenu.edu/writingcenter/grammar/sentencestructure

Here is a website offering you a clear definition of varying sentence structures and types of sentences. Also, Walden university provides Writing Centre for students who need guides on English academic writing, so you are able to find some academic writing strategies from the website https://academicguides.waldenu.edu/writingcenter.

Group-Work Activities

Syntax studies the structures of words in sentences. In English, a complete sentence should be structurally complete, that is, it should contain at least a subject and a predicate. In form, it should begin with a capital letter and end with a full stop, or a question mark, or an exclamation mark.

1. How much do you know about Chinese sentence structures? Can you name any structures you are very familiar with?

2. Can you compare the sentence structures of English with those of Chinese? Are there any differences?

3. Can you compare the sentence structures of mandarin with those of any other Chinese dialects?

Try to visit this website to find some ideas: https://chiculture.org.hk/sc/china-five-thousand-years/2065.

5.7 Deep Structure and Surface Structure

DEEP STRUCTURE
↓
Application of rules
↓
SURFACE STRUCTURE

Under the Chomskyan conception of syntax, when we first generate a sentence mentally, the constituents are often in a different order from when we pronounce the sentence. That is, there is a deep structure and a surface structure.

The deep structure is an abstract level of structural organization in which all the elements determining structural interpretation are represented.

(a) sentences that have alternative interpretations

(b) sentences that have different surface forms but the same underlying meaning.

The surface structure is how the sentence is actually represented. Sentences as they are formed at the level of deep structure are altered into their surface structure form via changes in the order of constituents called *transformation*s. For this reason, Chomsky's syntactic framework was, in earlier stages, called *transformational grammar.*

We have already seen one transformation: the placement of auxiliaries first in questions. It is relative intuitive that a sentence like *Is Bill walking*? is an inversion of a sentence *Bill is walking*. In "tree" terms, the auxiliary is moved to the front.

Traces are a less intuitive kind of transformation. An example is a sentence with what, like *What do you want to see?* Notice that you can use the *wanna* contraction in this sentence: *What do you wanna see?* Now, take the sentence *Who do you want to win the game?* Here, you would not use *wanna*, like *Who do you wanna win the game?* It sounds odd.

Under the transformational grammar conception, the reason for this is that in the deep structure what begins at the end of the sentence is moved to the beginning in the surface structure. The original sentence, then, would be *You want to see what?* There are three relevant facts: (a) In *What do you wanna see?* *what* is the object of *see*, which gives some reason for thinking that on some level what actually comes after its verb. (b) It is possible to phrase the question with *what* at the end: *You want to see what?* (c) There are many languages where words like *what* do not move to the front, such as Indonesian.

If *what* or *who* is moved to the beginning of the sentence, then we can presume that it leaves behind an empty slot at the end of the sentence. This is called a *trace*.

Evidence that traces really exist reveals itself when we look at *Who do you want to win the game?* Here, *who* is the subject of the subordinate clause. This would mean that the original sentence in deep structure is *You want who to win the game?* Note that one could even say it that way. If *who* left behind an empty slot, however, then this would explain why we do not say *Who do you wanna win the game?* There is a trace intervening between *want* and *to* in this case, such that a contraction cannot happen.

The trace conception is one of several phantom aspects of syntax, which under the Chomskyan conception are seen to be under the surface and not intuitive to ordinary speakers. Quite typically there are traces or nodes imperceptible except via analysis like the *wanna* contraction case.

Learning and Research Resources

- ***Syntax* (Journal)**
https://onlinelibrary.wiley.com/journal/14679612
Syntax is a peer-reviewed academic journal in the field of syntax of natural languages, established in 1998 and published by Wiley-Blackwell. It

is a journal covering the categories related to *Language and Linguistics* (Q1); *Linguistics and Language* (Q1). According to SCImago Journal Rank (SJR), this journal is ranked 1.361. *Syntax* has an h-index of 19. ISSN of this journal is/are 13680005. The impact factor of *Syntax* is 0.88.

● **National Geographic Learning**

https://ngllife.com/content/reading-texts-word

National Geographic Learning provides all English learners a place where you can download word versions of all the life reading texts. These reading texts can be good materials to explore phrases and sentence structure.

Summary

In this chapter, we've learned some concepts proposed by Noam Chomsky. And we've known how to categorise words according to their behaviours, i.e., which categories are open to new members, and which categories are not. Besides, we've learned about the difference between the deep structure and the surface structure.

Learning Highlights: Read and Think—Linguistics and Life

Syntax is systematically classified as a part of sentence. It is the set of rules, principles, and processes that govern the structure of sentences (sentence structure) in a given language, usually including word order. Also, we studied it in this chapter from different categories of words to distinct types of sentences.

1. How do you understand syntax as a set of rules?

2. What particular rules are you concerned with when you are generating a sentence?

Grammar (morphology, syntax) is the collection of rules governing the modification of words and their combination into sentences. It is therefore thanks to grammar that it becomes possible for language to invest man's thoughts in a material linguistic integument.

The distinguishing feature of grammar is that it gives rules for the modification of words not in reference to concrete words, but to words in

5 Syntax

general, not taken concretely; that it gives rules for the formation of sentences not in reference to particular concrete sentences, with, let us say, a concrete subject, a concrete predicate, etc., but to all sentences in general, irrespective of the concrete form of any sentence in particular. Hence, abstracting itself, as regards both words and sentences, from the particular and concrete, grammar takes that which is common and basic in the modification of words and their combination into sentences and builds it into grammatical rules, grammatical laws. Grammar is the outcome of a process of abstraction performed by the human mind over a long period of time; it is an indication of the tremendous achievement of thought.

1. How do you understand "Grammar is the outcome of a process of abstraction performed by the human mind?"
2. Do you think grammar may influence the human mind?

A general statement of irregularity and the human condition comes from the novelist Marguerite Yourcenar: Grammar, with its mixture of logical rule and arbitrary usage, proposes to a young mind a foretaste of what will be offered to him later on by law and ethics, those sciences of human conduct, and by all the systems wherein man has codified his instinctive experience.

Native speakers of a language learn correct syntax without realizing it. For example, phrase structure rules, proposed by Chomsky, are a type of rewritten rule used to describe a given language's syntax and are closely associated with the early stages of transformational grammar.
1. In what kind of circumstance was grammar produced?
2. Do you think grammatical system of language undergoes changes? Can you cite one case as an example?

The grammatical system of a language changes even more slowly than its basic word stock. Elaborated in the course of epochs, and having become part of the flesh and blood or the language, the grammatical system changes still more slowly than the basic word stock. With the lapse of time it, of course, undergoes changes, becomes more perfected, improves its rules, makes them more specific and acquires new rules; but the fundamentals of the grammatical system are preserved for a very long time, since, as history shows, they are able to serve society effectively through a succession of epochs. Hence, grammatical system and basic word stock constitute the foundation of language, the essence of its specific character.

Research Fronts

● Robert J. Hartsuiker and Sarah Bernlet did a research about how late second language learners learn the syntax of a second language.

...We focus particularly on psycholinguistic studies using structural priming (Bock, 1986). We then present a reanalysis of data collected by Schoonbaert, Hartsuiker and Pickering (2007), that bears upon the question of how lexical-syntactic representations vary with second language (L2) proficiency. Next, we sketch our account of the development of L2 syntax, which extends an earlier account presented by Bernolet, Hartsuiker and Pickering (2013). This approach differs from other work in second language acquisition (SLA) research in the sense that it is based on relatively explicit and mechanistic theories of the stages and representations a speaker moves through when mapping a message onto a sentence (e.g., Pickering & Branigan, 1998). But it is important to point out that our view has much in common with emergentist perspectives on language acquisition (e.g., O'Grady, Kwak, Lee & Lee, 2011) that try to understand acquisition phenomena in terms of frequency of exposure and difficulty of processing.

Their research concluded three phases:

(a) an initial phase without L2 syntactic representations; speakers transfer from the L1 during this phase and imitate native speakers;

(b) an intermediate phase, during which L2-specific nodes are formed;

(c) a final phase, when the L2-specific nodes have been merged with L1-specific nodes whenever this is possible, to form language-independent nodes.

Self-Study Activities

1. What is syntax?

2. What are words categories/classes? What are the differences between open class categories and closed categories?

3. What are head and modifiers?

4. What are deep structure and surface structure?

5. In the examples below, identify all main and subordinate clauses.

(1) Sunzi, who lived in China during the Spring and Autumn Period, is regarded as the ultimate master of war.

(2) Laozi told Kong Qiu that a saint should act like flowing water.

(3) Chinese scholars treat Zhu as their spiritual support, saying that they could live without eating meat but not without Zhu growing around their houses.

6. If you define a verb as being a word that expresses "action" or "a state of being," is your definition notional or formal?

7. In the sentence "The weather has been awful lately", why does "The weather" have the form of a noun phrase and the function of subject?

8. Identify the head words in the phrases below.

(1) the Chinese traditional festivals that contains Dragon Boat Festival

(2) very rapidly

(3) somewhat happy

(4) might have wished

(5) in the heat of the summer

(6) farmers hoping for rain

9. Please compare the following two pieces of Chinese poems and explore the differences between their structures and between their meanings?

（1）红帘映月昏黄近，冉冉浓香引。
　　绿芜空院小栏疏，对影悄妆残粉薄凝肤。
　　珑玲凤鬟圆环玉，索络虫钗扑。
　　露珠风冷逼窗梧，雨细隔灯寒梦倚楼孤。

（2）红帘映月昏黄近，冉冉浓香引绿芜。
　　空院小栏疏对影，悄妆残粉薄凝肤。
　　珑玲凤鬟圆环玉，索络虫钗扑露珠。
　　风冷逼窗梧雨细，隔灯寒梦倚楼孤。

10. Can you find any differences between Putonghua and Cantonese from the following sentences/words? Do you agree that some Cantonese sentences share the same sentence structure with English?

Putonghua	Cantonese
你先吃。	你食先。
找不到你。	搵你唔到。
对不起你。	对你唔住。
给你一块钱。	俾一蚊过你。
我给你送礼物。	我送礼物俾你。

Putonghua	Cantonese	Putonghua	Cantonese
素质	质素	粉汤	汤粉
夜宵	宵夜	秋千	千秋
责怪	怪责	客人	人客
要紧	紧要	干菜	菜干
公鸡	鸡公	底下	下底
粉汤	汤粉	裤袜	袜裤

Putonghua	Cantonese	English
你先走。	你行先。	You go first。
我比你大。	我大过你。	I am elder than you。

(1) Do you know any other dialects?

(2) In what ways are they different from Mandarin?

(3) Can you illustrate their differences with some examples?

11. Please read this poem and its Chinese versions. Which Chinese version has the similar structure with that of the original English poem?

You say that you love rain, 　　你说你爱雨，
but you open your umbrella when it rains. 　　但当细雨飘洒时，
　　你却撑开了伞；
You say that you love the sun, 　　你说你爱太阳，
but you find a shadow spot when the sun shines. 　　但日照当空时，
　　你却看见了阳光下的暗影。
You say that you love the wind, 　　你说你爱风，
but you close your windows when wind blows. 　　但当它轻拂时，
　　你却紧紧地关上了自己的窗子。
This is why I am afraid, 　　你说你也爱我，
you say that you love me too. 　　而我却为此烦恼。

12. Can you analyse the recursion in the following sentences?

吉尼斯世界纪录因记录了最多吉尼斯世界纪录被吉尼斯世界纪录纪录为纪录吉尼斯世界纪录最多的吉尼斯世界纪录。

转发《自治区教育厅办公室关于转发＜教育部关于做好春夏季中小学生和幼儿安全工作的紧急通知＞的通知》的通知。

Further Reading

A good introduction to Noam Chomsky's theory of generative grammar can be found in Steven Pinker's *The Language Instinct: How the Mind Creates Language* (New York: Harper Perennial Modern Classics, 2007).

The best way to find information on English syntax is to consult one of the major reference grammars of English: Randolph Quirk et al's *A Comprehensive Grammar of the English Language* (London: Longman, 1985), or Rodney Huddleston and Geoffrey K. Pullum's *The Cambridge Grammar of the English Language* (Cambridge: Cambridge University Press, 2002).

Douglas Biber et al.'s *Longman Grammar of Spoken and Written English* (Harlow, England: Pearson Education Limited, 1999) is corpus-based, and provides both descriptive information about English syntax and the frequency with which various syntactic constructions occur in registers of spoken and written English.

The information in each of the above grammars is also available in shorter, more pedagogically oriented textbook: Sidney Greenbaum and Randolph Quirk's *A Student's Grammar of the English Language* (London: Longman, 1990).

Outline

I. In the 1940s, Noam Chomsky (1928-) began to develop a theory under which all languages have a basic syntactic configuration that we are mentally hardwired to learn and use.

A. Chomsky first inaugurated this idea in what was published in 1957 as

Syntactic Structures. Within 10 years, this approach to syntax became the dominant one in linguistics, and it is taught universally today.

B. Chomsky's basic idea was that this process is innate, and he called it *universal grammar*.

II. **Syntax** studies the rules of using words in speech. It is part of grammar which investigates the act of producing speech utterances and utterances themselves.

III. Syntactic categories, which you might think of as "parts of speech", group words that behave similarly into similar categories.

A. Quirk, Greenbaum, Leech and Svartvik (1985) established the model of word class categorization.

B. Nouns, full verbs, adjectives and adverbs are often referred to as **open classes** because the number of words they comprise is not restricted and new members can constantly be added. The number of prepositions, pronouns, determiners, conjunctions, however, is limited and not easily subject to change. These word classes are thus called **closed classes**.

C. There are five commonly occurring types of phrase in English: noun phrases, adjective phrases, verb phrases, adverb phrases, and preposition phrases.

D. The clause is a much more clearly definable unit of linguistic analysis than the sentence. A clause can occur as a **dependent (or subordinate) clause** or an **independent clause.**

    i) Noun clauses

    ii) Adjective clauses

    iii) Adverbial clause

Sentences can exist independently, do not rely on any other unit and can be interpreted without reference to any other piece of language. Each sentence is an independent linguistics form, not included by virtue of any grammatical construction in any larger linguistic form.

    i) Simple sentences

    ii) Compound sentences

    iii) Complex sentences

    iv) Compound-complex sentences

F. A sentence can consist of one or more clauses; a clause can consist of one or more phrases; a phrase can consist of one or more words; and a word can consist of one or more morphemes.

G. Chomsky proposed that the base order of the sentence is the **deep structure** and that derived orders (derived by the application of movement rules such as SAI) are **surface structures**.

H. Sentences as they are formed at the level of deep structure are altered into their surface-structure form via changes in the order of constituents called **transformations.**

   i) *Traces* are a less intuitive kind of transformation.

6 Semantics

6.1 Introduction

Human being's languages differ from the communication systems of other animals in being stimulus-free and creative. Early in life every human acquires the essentials of a language—vocabulary and pronunciation, use and meaning of each item in it. The speaker's knowledge is largely implicit. The linguist attempts to construct a grammar, an explicit description of the language, the categories of the language and the rules by which they interact. Semantics is one part of the grammar; phonology, syntax and morphology are other parts, which studies how to convey meaning in all of its shades.

In this chapter, we will focus on the semantic level of how we use language in addition to phonetics, phonology, morphology, and syntax. We have already come across the word "semantic" in previous chapters. Semantics is the systematic study of meaning, and linguistic semantics is the study of how languages organize and express meanings. Linguistic semantics is an attempt to explicate the knowledge of any speaker of a language which allows that speaker to communicate facts, feelings, intentions and products of the imagination to other speakers and to understand what they communicate to him or her.

6.2 Semantic Roles

In linguistic theory, semantic roles have traditionally been regarded as determinant in expressing generalizations about the syntactic realization of a predicate's arguments. Semantic roles show how syntactic concepts of subject and object can only take us so far. For example, *Chinese created calligraphy* and *Calligraphy was created by Chinese* express the same concept. Both have a subject. However, the subjects in the two sentences are different entities. There is a separate level of grammar distinct from grammatical roles like subject and object. Linguists say that in both of these sentences, *Chinese* is the **agent** while *calligraphy* is the **patient**. These are termed **semantic roles**. Not all subjects in active sentences are agents. In *People expressed their grief to the tragedy caused by the diease*, the subject is not an agent but has the semantic role termed **experiencer**. The noun within the prepositional phrase of a passive sentence is not necessarily an agent. In *Harold got hit by a rock*, *rock* is a cause. In *Harold got hit with a rock*, the rock is an **instrument**. In the same way, in *The rock knocked him out*, rock is a **cause**, while in *The key will open that door, key* is an instrument. Table 6.1 gives definitions and illustrations for all semantic roles.

Table 6.1 Semantic roles

actor	The role of an argument that performs some action without affecting any other entity.	*Andrew left.*
affected	The role of an argument that undergoes a change due to some event or is affected by some other entity.	*A window broke.* *Tom broke a window.* *Betty likes Peking Opera.* *Peking Opera delights Betty.*
affecting	The role of an argument that, without any action, affects another entity.	*Betty likes Peking Opera.* *Peking Opera delights Betty.*
agent	The role of an argument that by its action affects some other entity.	*Tom broke a window.*
associate	The role of an argument that tells the status or identity of another argument, the **theme**.	*Roger is a student.*
effect	The role of an argument that comes into existence through the action of the predicate.	*Tillie baked a pie.*
place	The role of an argument that names the location in which the action of the predicate occurs.	*The fireman climbed a ladder.*
theme	The role of an argument that is the topic of a predicate that does not express action—a stative predicate.	*Audrey is a computer expert.*

6.3 Semantic Relations

6.3.1 Semantic Fields

Another thing we know about word meaning is that words can be divided into semantic categories called **semantic fields**. Semantic fields are classifications of words associated by their meanings. There is a great deal of evidence that words are stored in semantic fields in our mental dictionaries. Semantic fields could be clothing, parts of the body, emotions, old boyfriends; the fields may vary across speakers, and words may belong to more than one category. The meaning of the word *pig* in the semantic field of farm animals overlaps the meaning in the semantic field of meat and even (possibly) pets.

Slips of the tongue provide interesting evidence for semantic fields. The word substituted for the intended word in the following slips of the tongue is a semantically related one:

Intended Utterance	Actual Utterance
he's going *up* town	he's going *down* town
you have too many irons in the *fire*	*They* have too many irons in the *smoke*
that's a horse of another *colour*	that's a horse of another *race*

The semantic field including both *up* and *down* might be directions; for *fire* and *smoke*, things having to do with fire, and so on. Speakers rarely, if ever, make random substitutions when producing a slip of the tongue (though we know from other chapters that some slips are phonetic, some phonological, and some morphological, as well as semantic). In addition to slips of the tongue, aphasia provides us with evidence of how words might be stored in the brain.

6.3.2 Semantic Relations

Semanticists have compared words in terms of a group of more general semantic relations that describe various degrees of similarities and differences that words exhibit. There are twelve different relations that have been proposed, including the three: ***antonymy, synonymy*** and ***hyponymy.***

Opposite Meanings: Antonymy

We all learn, early on, that *rich* is the opposite of *poor*, *awake* is the opposite of *asleep*, and *teacher* is the opposite of *student*. These opposites, or antonyms, seem based on fact: if you are rich, you can't be poor; if you are awake, you can't be asleep; and in class, the "opposite" roles of teacher and student seem well defined and obvious. (If you ask someone what the opposite of *pepper* is, they'll probably say *salt*.)

Nevertheless, there are important differences among these pairs. Some antonyms are **gradable**; that is, the antonyms are two ends on a scale, and there can be various gradations of each term. So, what is considered rich or poor varies from person to person. What *rich* means to Tevye in the musical *Fiddler on the Roof* as he sings "If I Were a Rich Man" is quite different from what *rich* means to Bill Gates; for someone who used to weigh 300 pounds, weighing 200 pounds might be a blessing. Antonyms therefore express degree in various ways: by comparative and superlative morphology (smarter, thinner) or syntactically (more gigantic, extremely minuscule).

Complementary antonyms are another subtype of antonymy: if you are one, you cannot be the other; these are "absolute" opposites. That is, if you are *dead*, you cannot also be *alive*; if you are *asleep*, you are not *awake*, and so on. Similar pairs of this sort include *legal/illegal* and *begin/end*.

Relational antonyms are a third type; these are pairs in which each member describes a relationship to the other: *teacher/student, father/mother, lawyer/client, doctor/patient*. All languages have antonyms as well as these subtypes of antonyms (see Table 6.2).

Table 6.2 Antonym Types

Gradable	Relational	Complementary
smart/stupid	teacher/student	dead/alive
often/rarely	friend/enemy	before/after
fat/thin	question/answer	permit/prohibit
most/least	doctor/patient	precede/follow
up/down	mother/father	send/receive
tall/short	parent/child	beginning/end
rich/poor	lawyer/client	day/night

Synonym: Bilateral Entailment

Words that are different in form but similar in meaning are called synonyms. Synonyms are derived from a variety of sources, and we make choices among synonyms for a variety of reasons. One source of synonyms is dialectal variation. In some dialects of North American English, a long, upholstered seat is called a couch, but speakers of another dialect call the same piece of furniture a sofa. Canadian English speakers might call this item a chesterfield, and still other speakers might call it a divan. Though these words all mean the same thing and are therefore synonyms, they tend to be dialect specific and may not be shared across dialect boundaries. Synonyms can also cross dialect boundaries; most North American English speakers are familiar with the following synonyms: professor/instructor, doctor/physician, and lawyer/attorney. Still other synonyms arise as a result of language change over time. For example, your grandparents might use a particular term that seems old fashioned to you, and you might use a more modern term. For example, what might be a pocketbook for your grandmother is called in current fashion circles a handbag or a bag or a purse. An older term for dress is frock, and what used to be called a baby carriage or perambulator is now a stroller or jogger; we are less likely now to refer to women as gals. Two other, closely related sources for synonyms are style and register. In casual speech, a speaker might say, "That's a nice ride," but in more formal speech, "That's a nice car." For a variety of historical reasons, we attach social value and prestige to words with Latin or Greek roots. We therefore might choose a Latinate synonym over its native English (Anglo-Saxon) counterpart in formal, academic writing. Table 6.3 shows some pairs of synonyms or at least close synonyms (Exact synonyms are quite rare.).

Table 6.3 Synonyms of Anglo-Saxon and Latin/Greek Origin

Anglo-Saxon Origin	Latin/Greek Origin
land	alight
try	attempt
hard	difficult
talk (about)	discuss
crazy	insane
ghost	spirit

Anglo-Saxon Origin	Latin/Greek Origin
clean	sanitary
dirt	soil
go	advance
see	visualize
holy	sacred
space	cosmos
heavenly	celestial

Learning and Research Resources

● **Thesaurus**

https://www.thesaurus.com/

Thesaurus.com is a free website for finding synonyms and antonyms of words. They are often used by writers to help find the best word to express an idea.

● **Visuwords**

https://visuwords.com/

Visuwords is a visualization tool based upon Princeton University's WordNet. The online graphical database—part dictionary, part thesaurus—groups words by their meanings and associations with other words and concepts. These related linguistic ideas are visually displayed in an interactive graphic.

Group-Work Activities

The Nameless is the origin of Heaven and Earth;
The Named is the Mother of All Things.
Therefore: Often times, one strips oneself of passion.
In order to see the Secret of Life;
Often times, one regards life with passion, in order to see its manifest forms.
These two (the Secret and its manifestations) are (in their nature) the same;
They are given different names when they become manifest.

名可名，非恒名。
无名天地之始；有名万物之母。
故常无欲，以观其妙；常有欲，以观其徼。
此两者同出而异名……

(选自《道德经》林语堂 译本)

1. How do you understand "These two (the Secret and its manifestations) are (in their nature) the same; They are given different names when they become manifest."?

2. "The Secret" and "its manifestations" are not synonyms. Why did Laozi claim that they were the same thing with different names?

Euphemisms

English has a vast number of synonyms, more than most languages, largely because of borrowing from other languages, especially French and Latin. Though synonymy allows for a variety of ways to express ideas, it can also be the source of euphemisms. Euphemisms are words and phrases used to avoid offending (by directly addressing taboo subjects) or to deliberately obscure actual (usually unpleasant) meanings. Government terminology provides a good source of examples. Area denial munitions are "landmines", and physical persuasion means "torture". Operational exhaustion means "shell shock", and wet work is "assassination". We use euphemisms to avoid talking about bodily functions: *sweat* can be replaced by *perspire*, *genitalia* by *privates*, and *urinate* by *go to the bathroom*.

Still another source of synonyms is **politically correct language**, terminology specifically intended to limit use of certain terms in favour of more socially and culturally acceptable ones in public discussion. Common examples include *Native American* for *Indian*, *firefighter* for *fireman*, *differently abled* rather than *disabled* or *handicapped*, and *mail carrier* rather than *mailman*. The use of politically correct language can be the source of some controversy because politically correct terms can be—not surprisingly—political, which raises questions about the accuracy of their meanings and the implications of those meanings.

6 Semantics

Hyponymy: Unilateral Entailment

One of the central semantic relations that can be taken as an indication of the structuredness of vocabulary is hyponymy. Hyponymy expresses how we assign meaning to larger categories and to smaller categories included in these larger ones. We use hyponymy in language to make general statements more specific: *What are you eating?* and *Dumplings/Hot Pot/ Biangbiang noodles.*

So *Dumplings, hot pot,* and *Biangbiang noodles* are all hyponyms of *Chinese food*. In turn, *Chinese food* is a hyponym of *food*.

Also, *pigeon, crow, eagle* and *seagull* are all hyponyms of *bird*. In turn, *bird* is a hyponym of *animal*.

6.3.3 Polysemy

The same morphological word may have a range of different meanings as a glance at any dictionary will reveal. **Polysemy**, meaning "many meanings", is the name given to the study of this particular phenomenon. Polysemy is the association of one word with two or more distinct meanings, and a polyseme is a word or phrase with multiple meanings. The word "polysemy" comes from the Greek for "many signs." The adjective forms of the word include polysemous or polysemic.

In a dictionary entry for any given word the meanings are listed in a particular order with the central meaning given first, followed by the most closely related meanings and with metaphorical extensions coming last.

In theory, the idea of words having several meanings is straight-forward; in practice there are problems, especially in relation to drawing boundary lines between words. It is not always easy to decide when a meaning has become so different from its original meaning that it deserves to be treated like a new word. In *Concise Oxford Dictionary*, for example, *pupil* has two meanings:

(a) One who is taught by another, scholar

(b) Circular opening in centre of iris of eye regulating passage of light to the retina

Many speakers of English, however, regard these as two different words. Stated simply, the essential problem is that it is not always easy or even possible to be certain whether we are dealing with polysemy, which is one word with several meanings; or homonymy, which is several words with the same form.

Normally dictionaries decide between polysemy and homonymy by referring to etymology (the origins and history of a word) when this is known, but even this rule is not foolproof because, on occasions, etymologically related words may have different spellings as in the case of "flower" and "flour". The simplest solution is to seek a core of meaning and any homonymous items sharing the core should be classified as polysemous.

The phenomenon of polysemy is not restricted to full words in English. Multiplicity of meaning is a very general characteristic of language and is found in prefixes as well as full words. Let us take *un* for example. When it prefixes a verb, it usually means reverse the action of the verb; it can mean deprive of this noun: unhorse, unman (that is, deprive of manly qualities). This usage is rare in English now but previously words like unbishop, unduke, unking, unlord occurred. When *un* precedes an adjective, it can mean the opposite of: unfair, ungracious, unkind, untrue.

Group-Work Activities

在宋小宝的小品《吃面》中，宋小宝嫌炒面太干，说:"太干,换碗汤面。"吃完后服务员来结账——

服务员：汤面钱。

宋小宝：汤面我用炒面换的，给什么钱?

服务员：那炒面你也没给钱呐？

宋小宝：炒面我没吃给什么钱?

1. How does Song Xiaobao do the trick in this conversation?
2. Do they have the same interpretation of the word "换"?

6 Semantics

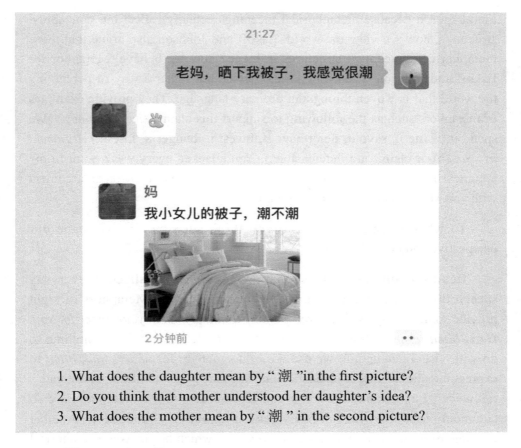

1. What does the daughter mean by "潮" in the first picture?
2. Do you think that mother understood her daughter's idea?
3. What does the mother mean by "潮" in the second picture?

6.4 Figurative Language

Figurative language refers to the use of words in a way that deviates from the conventional order and meaning in order to convey a complicated meaning, colourful writing, clarity, or evocative comparison. It uses an ordinary sentence to refer to something without directly stating it.

6.4.1 Connecting Meanings: Metaphor

Perhaps the most recognisable use of figurative language is **metaphor**. A metaphor, as Aristotle conceived it and as we still understand it, is a figure of speech that sets up an analogy between two words or phrases: **something is something else**. The word ultimately comes from the Greek *metaphero,* meaning "to carry over" or "transfer." As mentioned, Lakoff and Johnson (1980) take the position that there is no real distinction between metaphors and literal speech because metaphorical meanings actually reflect our conceptual structures, how we view the world. Lakoff and Johnson also argue that these metaphorical conceptual structures influence how we behave. Metaphor for Lakoff and Johnson is not a rhetorical device but rather a way of perceiving the world that is woven throughout ordinary language. They provide examples of metaphors such as the following to support this claim: *Time is money.* (We spend it, waste it, save it, don't have it, invest it, budget it, lose it.) *Argument as war.* (Your claims are indefensible.) (You attacked every weak point in my argument.) (Your criticisms were right on target.) (I''ve never won an argument with you.) (You shot down all my arguments.)

To what extent, if at all, do you think such metaphors shape our perspective and our behaviour?

Dead metaphors are those that are so conventionalized in everyday speech that we don't even realize they are metaphors. Metaphors of sight provide some examples: *I see your point. I'll take a look at your paper for you. He is blind to new ideas.* These uses of *see*, *look*, and *blind* have nothing to do with visual perception; we use *see* as a synonym for *understand*, *blind* to express intentional lack of understanding, and *take a look* to mean "investigate". (However, Lakoff and Johnson argue that because these metaphors are so commonly used, they are not really dead at all but very productive.) Another example of a truly dead metaphor is *broadcast*, which began as a metaphorical use of the casting of seeds broadly; today, it is not likely that anyone makes a connection with the spreading of seed. We do have to *learn* that these are dead, however, as evidenced by some children's use and understanding of these words. A child who overhears the sentence *He can be so blind sometimes* might ask, "Is he really blind?" And one child, knowing that *say* means "to utter", said about a sign: "The sign wrote . . ." rather than "The sign said . . ." She had not yet learned the metaphorical meaning of *say*.

Mixed metaphors are those in which parts of different metaphors are telescoped into one utterance. This mixing can occur for a variety of reasons. The following examples were taken from the University of Illinois at Chicago website (http://tigger.uic.edu/~rramakri/Readings/ Fun/Mixed-Metaphors.htm):

She grabbed the bull by the horns, and ran with it.

6 Semantics

I've hit the nail on the jackpot.
I'm shooting from the seat of my pants.
You're pulling my leg over my eyes.
I'm flying by the edge of my seat.
Beware my friend . . . you are skating on hot water.
I would not trust him with a ten-foot pole.
We're robbing
Peter to pay the piper.
I can see the carrot at the end of the tunnel.

We might come up with "hit the nail on the jackpot" because the two source metaphors ("hit the nail on the head" and "hit the jackpot") overlap in meaning ("to achieve a goal of some kind") and/or because they both include the verb *hit*. We might produce "flying by the edge of my seat" because both "flying by the seat of my pants" and "on the edge of my seat" have related meanings (unplanned action that may include fear and anxiety) and/ or because both metaphors include the word *seat*.

Personification, another subtype of metaphorical language, gives human attributes to something that is not human. (For some, there is overlap between personification and anthropomorphism, but others argue that anthropomorphism is more specific, ascribing human qualities to gods, while others believe anthropomorphism to be more general than just language use; for example, ascribing human characteristics to nonhuman form in art.)

The steeples swam in the mist.
The gates opened their arms.
The project ate up all my time.
The cold knocked me out.
The idea died a natural death.
His theory explained . . .
These facts suggest . . .

Synaesthesia is a type of metaphorical language in which one kind of sensation is described in terms of another (Colour is attributed to sounds, odour to colour, sound to odour, etc.). Examples include "sweet" smells (taste attributed to smell), "loud" colours (sound attributed to colour), and so on. In the following lines from Charles Baudelaire's poem "Correspondences," "perfumes" (smells) are described in terms of touch ("fresh like the skin of infants"). The sense of touch is described in terms of sound ("sweet like oboes"). Finally, perfumes are described in terms of colour ("green like prairies").

6.4.2 Metonymy

Another type of figurative speech is **metonymy**; we refer to something by describing it in terms of something with which it is closely associated. A well-known example of metonymy is "The pen is mightier than the sword", in which *pen* refers to writing or diplomacy and *sword* to action or war. Additional examples are the following: "*The Pentagon/The White House/Congress* issued a statement yesterday." and "*The law* is after her."

We often use metonymy to create verbs from nouns. They *limousined* to the prom last night. We *Taco Belled* for lunch today. **Synecdoche** is a specific type of metonymy in which we use a part of something to refer to the whole thing. A physician may refer to a patient as *the tonsillectomy* rather than *the patient in 4B or Mary Jones*. We may refer to a car as *wheels* or *a ride,* head as cattle, threads as clothing, skirt as woman, and suit as man. Sometimes synecdoche is more abstract:

Give me *a hand* = help
Lend me *an ear* = your attention
Two heads are better than one = cooperation

Synecdoche can also involve referring to something by the manufacturer, product, material, or colour.

I like my *Honda* = producer for product
Natural fibres are all the rage these days = cotton clothes
Do you take *plastic?* = credit cards

Some theorists suggest that all language is metonymic since words stand for things (See Lakoff 1987, for example.).

6.4.3 Comparing Meanings: Simile

Similes differ from metaphor and metonymy in that they involve a comparison of two unlike things and usually involve the words *like* or *as*.

He eats like a pig.
She's big as a house.
We're happy as clams.
My brain is like a sieve.

Here are some famous similes:

Suspicion climbed all over her face, like a kitten, but not so playfully. (Raymond Chandler)

Exuding good will like a mortician"s convention in a plague year. (Daniel Berrigan)

As good as gold. (Charles Dickens)

Death hangs on her like an untimely frost. (William Shakespeare)

Solitude . . . is like Spanish moss which finally suffocates the tree it hangs on. (Anaïs Nin)

A woman without a man is like a fish without a bicycle. (attributed to Gloria Steinem)

Learning and Research Resources

• **English Club—A list of English similes**
https://www.englishclub.com/vocabulary/figures-similes-list.htm
English Club is a free website designed to help you learn English online. You may find a list of common English similes here.

6.4.4 Idiom

Another type of figurative speech is **idiom**. Like other kinds of figurative language, idioms are collocations of words or phrases with nonliteral meanings. An idiom can be defined as a combination of two or more words which function as a unit of meaning or as a lexical complex which is semantically complex.

Idioms can take different forms, for instance:

(a) **noun phrases**: the wind of change, bad blood, a nervous wreck.

(b) **predicates**: have a frog in one's throat, have second thoughts, pull strings, scream blue murder.

(c) **sentences**: the early bird catches the worm, don't cry over spilt milk.

(d) **phrasal verbs** (combinations of verb and adverbial particle): look up, come up with.

Some idioms, especially phrases, have become common and even routine figures of speech. A couple of examples are *stand up for*, meaning "assert or insist on" as in *Stand up for your rights* (a case of metonymy, in which standing up is usually associated with but not otherwise similar to insistence or assertion); and necessity is the mother of invention (a case of metaphor, in which necessity "gives birth" to invention).

Many idioms become the customary way of expressing some meanings, and as a result have fully lost their sense of non-literalness. For example,

understand, literally "stand under"; metaphorically speaking, to become knowledgeable/aware of something is to "stand under" it.
run for "actively seek" political office; metaphorically speaking, actively to seek political office is to "run for office" like a runner for a prize.

Neither of these usages, as idioms, any longer has any novelty or demands interpretation as a figure of speech.

Learning and Research Resources

The Idioms

https://www.theidioms.com/

The Idioms is the largest English idiom dictionary, and you can find some common idioms on this website. Try to find the meaning of "apple of eye".

Group-Work Activities

"读庄子本分不出哪是思想的美，哪是文学的美。那思想与文字、外形与本质的极端的调和，那种不可捉摸的浑圆的机体，便是文学家的极致；只那一点，便足注定庄子在文学中的地位。"——闻一多《庄子》

"世界本无所谓真纯的思想，除了托身在文学里，思想别无存在的余地；同时，是一个字便有它的含义，文字等于是思想的躯壳。然而说来又觉得矛盾，一拿单字连缀成文章，居然有了缺乏思想的文字，或是文字表达不出的思想。比方我讲自然现象中有一种无光的火，你肯信吗？在人工的制作里确乎有那种文字与思想不碰头的偏枯的现象，不是词不达意，便是辞浮于理。"——闻一多《庄子》

1. Do you agree with Wen Yiduo that Zhungzi's essays are the beautiful combination of words and ideas? Can you give one example as illustration?
2. How do you understand the relationship between language and thought?
3. What is the harm if language and thought mismatch?

"势为天子，未必贵也；穷为匹夫，未必贱也。贵贱之分，在行之美丑。"——《庄子·杂篇·盗跖》

4. What makes a noble man? Do you agree with Zhungzi?

Here is the evidence of connection between language and thought.

"观念不能离开语言而存在。"——马克思《政治经济学批判》

"Language is a medium, an instrument with the help of which people

communicate with one another, exchange thoughts and understand each other. Being directly connected with thinking, language registers and fixes in words, and in words combined into sentences, the results of the process of thinking and achievements of man's cognitive activity, and thus makes possible the exchange of thoughts in human society."

——Joseph Stalin, *Marxism and Problems of Linguistics: Concerning Marxism in Linguistics*

"语言作为人们交际的工具、作为社会中交流思想的工具是为社会服务的,这个工具使人们能够相互了解并调整他们在人类社会活动的一切范围……中的共同工作。"

——斯大林《马克思主义和语言学问题——论语言学的几个问题》

"不论人的头脑会产生什么样的思想,以及这些思想什么时候产生,它们只有在语言材料的基础上、在语言的词和句的基础上才能产生和存在。"

——斯大林《马克思主义和语言学问题——论语言学的几个问题》

"句子感知模块是人类心智的一个代表性的固定结构,他负责逐字逐句地传递说话者心中的想法,而不被听者的偏见或期待干扰。无论人何时何地,这个模块都可以让人们在"何为正义""何为真实"的问题上达成一致,就仿佛它们是客观的实体,而不像口味、习俗和自我利益那样因人而异。"

——史蒂芬·平克《语言本能》

Summary

Semantics and pragmatics are the two main branches of the linguistic study of meaning. Semantics is the study of the "toolkit" for meaning: knowledge encoded in the vocabulary of the language and in its patterns for building more elaborate meanings, up to the level of sentence meanings. In the next chapter, we will focus on studying what is concerned in pragmatics area.

Learning Highlights: Read and Think—Linguistics and Life

- **The complexity of semantics**

Semantics is the study of the relationship between words and how we draw meaning from those words. Semantics involves the deconstruction of words, signals, and sentence structure. Semantic relationships are the associations that exist between the meanings of words (semantic relationships at word level), between the meanings of phrases, or between the meanings of sentences (semantic relationships at the phrase or sentence level).

1. Do you think it is a complex process drawing meaning from words? Why or why not?
2. Do people have the legitimacy of interpreting the meanings of words based on their personal understanding/attitudes? Why or why not?
3. How do people attach a different meaning to a word depending on class affinity?

Let us see how Joseph Stalin answer this question:

...you want to know whether classes influence language, whether they introduce into language their specific words and expressions, whether there are cases when people attach a different meaning to one and the same word or expression depending on their class affinity?

Yes, classes influence language, introduce into the language their own specific words and expressions and sometimes understand one and the same word or expression differently. There is no doubt about that. However, it does not follow that specific words and expressions, as well as difference in semantics, can be of serious importance for the development of a single language common to the whole people, that they are capable of detracting from its significance or of changing its character. Firstly, such specific words and expressions, as well as cases of difference in semantics, are so few in language that they hardly make up even one percent of the entire linguistic material. Consequently, all the remaining overwhelming mass of words and expressions, as well as their semantics, are common to all classes of society.

Secondly, specific words and expressions with a class tinge are used in speech not according to rules of some sort of "class" grammar, which does not exist, but according to the grammatical rules of the existing language common to the whole people.

Hence, the existence of specific words and expressions and the facts of differences in the semantics of language do not refute, but, on the contrary, confirm the existence and necessity of a single language common to the whole people.

4. Do you agree with him that classes do influence language?

Let us see how Karl Marx interpreted the complexity of meaning:

……对于语言表达中的那些极其细微的差别,即使要做出毫无把握的判断,恐怕也是不可能的。

Marx's words remind us of the individuality of semantic studies. Since semantics is closely linked to the subjects of representation, reference and denotation, people can absolutely interpret words differently and draw different meanings from them. Semantics influences our reading comprehension as well as our comprehension of other people's words in everyday conversation, and it plays a large part in our daily communication, understanding, and language learning without us even realizing it. This is also why we consider semantics is complex because it is largely about the exploration of the depths of our consciousness.

Research Fronts

Elizabeth D. Peña, Lisa M. Bedore, Mirza J. Lugo-Neris and Nahar Albudoor did a research about identifying developmental language disorder in school age bilinguals. They argue that "children with developmental language disorder (DLD) have particular difficulty learning language despite otherwise general normal development."

... Educators share the responsibility for ensuring the students in their classrooms have the best possible educational outcomes. Students who are

6 Semantics

English learners (ELs) are at risk for poor educational outcomes when they lack the linguistic foundations needed for literacy and to gain access to the academic content presented across subject areas ...

Their works shows what kinds of measures might work to different bilingual children.

...Children in the low proficiency group were particularly likely to persist in the low group although they had language experiences comparable to those children who demonstrated increased proficiency. The investigators obtained information about children's referral to speech and language services. Less than half of the children in the low proficient group received speech and language services and even those children did not shift out of the low proficiency group. The authors highlight the need to take a more proactive stance in identifying bilingual children who may have language-learning difficulties such as DLD. (developmental language disorder)...

Self-Study Activities

1. What are semantic fields?
2. What is polysemy? Explain it with examples.
3. What is metaphor? How is it different from simile?
4. What are the semantic features that *bull* and *man* share? What semantic features distinguish them from one another?
5. Is it possible for two words to be completely synonymous? Illustrate your answers with examples.
6. Match the word groups in the left-hand column with the semantic relation in the right-hand column with which each group would be associated.

(1) bee/mosquito	(a) synonyms
(2) hot/cold	(b) co-hyponyms
(3) help/assist	(c) antonyms
(4) anthropology/sociology	
(5) guilty/innocent	
(6) warm/tepid	

7. Can you analyse the meaning of "弄" and "刷" in the following sentences?

（1）这个锅有点脏，你赶紧弄干净。
（2）头发分叉了，下午去理发店弄下。
（3）电脑蓝屏了，弄了好久也没弄好。
（4）今天在家大扫除，弄了一身灰。
（5）心情有点不好，别惹我，不然弄你。
（6）没事浏览下网站是"刷网站"。
（7）班里的学霸做题是"刷题"。
（8）重复考六级是"刷分"。
（9）遇到特好看的电影，看了几遍就是"几刷"。
（10）运气爆棚就全靠"刷人品"。
（11）网上的商家最喜欢"刷信誉"。

Further Reading

General introductions to linguistic semantics are numerous. The following can be recommended for the beginner who wants collateral or supplemental reading in the subject:

Allan, Keith (1986). *Linguistic Meaning* (2 vols); Dillon, George (1977). *Introduction to Contemporary Linguistic Semantics*; Hofmann, Th. R. (1993). *Realms of Meaning: An Introduction to Semantics*; Herford, J.R. and Brendan Heasley (1983). *Semantics: A Coursebook.*

The more advanced student may be interested in:

Chierchia, Gennaro and Sally McConnell-Ginet (1990). *Meaning and Grammar: An Introduction to Semantics*; Frawley, William (1992). *Linguistic Semantics*; Kempson, R.M. (1977). *Semantic Theory*.

A lexicographical perspective on lexical semantics is presented in M. L. Murphy's *Semantic Relations and the Lexicon* (Cambridge: Cambridge University Press, 2003). The WordNet database is discussed in *WordNet: An Electronic Lexical Database* edited by C. Fellbaum (Cambridge, MA: MIT Press, 1998).

6 Semantics

A cross-linguistic description of semantic primitives is outlined in A. Wierzbicka's, *Semantics: Primes and Universals* (Oxford: Oxford University Press, 1996).

Outline

I. Semantics is the systematic study of meaning, and linguistic semantics is the study of how languages organize and express meanings.

II. Linguistic semantics is an attempt to explicate the knowledge of any speaker of a language which allows that speaker to communicate facts, feelings, intentions and products of the imagination to other speakers and to understand what they communicate to him or her.

III. A proposition is something abstract but meaningful. It can be expressed in different sentences and in parts of sentences, perhaps with differences of focus but always with the same basic meaning. A proposition can be expressed in different sentences.

IV. An English sentence has certain kinds of modification that, together, we call **inflection**. Inflection includes **tense** (the distinction between present *celebrate* and past *celebrated*, for instance), **aspect** (*are celebrating, have celebrated*), and **modality** (*may celebrate, could celebrate, should celebrate*, among other possibilities).

V. Syntactic analysis is about the description of a sentence, while semantic analysis is about the description of a proposition.

   A. A syntactic analysis is an account of the lexemes and function words in a sentence, describing how they combine into phrases, and showing the functions that these lexemes and phrases have in the sentence.

   B. The semantic analysis deals with meaning, the proposition expressed in the sentence, not necessarily including all the function words in the sentence.

VI. **Semantic roles** show how syntactic concepts of subject and object can only take us so far.

   A. **Actor**: The role of an argument that performs some action without affecting any other entity.

   B. **Affecting**: The role of an argument that, without any action, affects another entity.

C. **Affected**: The role of an argument that undergoes a change due to some event or is affected by some other entity.

D. **Agent**: The role of an argument that by its action affects some other entity.

E. **Associate:** The role of an argument that tells the status or identity of another argument, the **theme.**

F. **Effect**: The role of an argument that comes into existence through the action of the predicate.

G. **Place**: The role of an argument that names the location in which the action of the predicate occurs.

H. **Theme**: The role of an argument that is the topic of a predicate that does not express action—a stative predicate.

Ⅶ. **Semantic fields** are classifications of words associated by their meanings. There is a great deal of evidence that words are stored in semantic fields in our mental dictionaries. Semantic fields could be clothing, parts of the body, emotions, old boyfriends; the fields may vary across speakers, and words may belong to more than one category.

Ⅷ. Semantic relations describe various degrees of similarities and differences that words exhibit.

A. **Antonymy,** simply means opposite meanings.

ⅰ) Some antonyms are **gradable**; that is, the antonyms are two ends on a scale, and there can be various gradations of each term. e.g. *poor/rich*.

ⅱ) **Complementary antonyms** are another subtype of antonymy: if you are one, you cannot be the other; these are "absolute" opposites. e.g. *dead/alive; awake/asleep.*

ⅲ) **Relational antonyms** are pairs in which each member describes a relationship to the other. e.g. *teacher/student, father/mother, lawyer/client, doctor/patient.*

B. Words that are different in form but similar in meaning are called **synonyms.**

ⅰ) Though synonymy allows for a variety of ways to express ideas, it can also be the source of euphemisms. **Euphemisms** are words and phrases used to avoid offending. e.g. urinate—bathroom.

ⅱ) Another source of synonyms is **politically correct language**, terminology specifically intended to limit use of certain terms in favour of more socially and culturally acceptable ones in public discussion.

C. **Hyponymy** expresses how we assign meaning to larger categories and to smaller categories included in these larger ones. We use hyponymy in language to make general statements more specific.

IX. **Polysemy** simply means "many meanings"; however, it is not always easy to decide when a meaning has become so different from its original meaning that it deserves to be treated like a new word. For example, the word *pupil* has two meanings: one who is taught by another, scholar; circular opening in centre of iris of eye regulating passage of light to the retina.

X. How a language splits up or points at reality is called the **deictic** aspect of semantics. The word deixis comes from the Greek word for pointing. For example, **spatial deixis** involves pointing out how close or how far things are from us.

XI. **Figurative language** refers to the use of words in a way that deviates from the conventional order and meaning in order to convey a complicated meaning, colourful writing, clarity, or evocative comparison. It uses an ordinary sentence to refer to something without directly stating it.

A. A metaphor is a figure of speech that sets up an analogy between two words or phrases: *something is something else.*

ⅰ) **Dead metaphors** are those that are so conventionalized in everyday speech that we don't even realize they are metaphors.

ⅱ) **Mixed metaphors** are those in which parts of different metaphors are telescoped into one utterance.

ⅲ) **Personification**, another subtype of metaphorical language, gives human attributes to something that is not human.

ⅳ) **Synaesthesia** is a type of metaphorical language in which one kind of sensation is described in terms of another (Colour is attributed to sounds, odour to colour, sound to odour, etc.).

B. **Metonymy** refers to something by describing it in terms of something with which it is closely associated. We often use metonymy to create verbs from nouns. e.g. Give me *a hand* = Help.

C. **Similes** differ from metaphor and metonymy in that they involve a comparison of two unlike things and usually involve the words *like* or *as*.

D. An **idiom** can be defined as a combination of two or more words which function as a unit of meaning or as a lexical complex which is semantically simplex.

7   Pragmatics

7.1   Introduction

This chapter explores how the social context in which language is used affects human communication. It begins with a discussion of five linguistic situations requiring pragmatics. The next sections describe how utterances are used and structured in human communication, starting with speech act theory, a theory that formalizes the notion that what people actually intend their utterances to mean is often not clearly spelled out in the words that they speak or write.

Pragmatics is another branch of linguistics that is concerned with meaning. Pragmatics and semantics can be viewed as different parts, or different aspects, of the same general study. Both are concerned with people's ability to use language meaningfully. While semantics is mainly concerned with a speaker's competence to use the language system in producing meaningful utterances and processing (comprehending) utterances produced by others, the chief focus of pragmatics is a person's ability to derive meanings from specific kinds of speech situations—to recognize what the speaker is referring to, to relate new information to what has gone before, to interpret what is said from background knowledge about the speaker and the topic of discourse, and to infer or "fill in" information that the speaker takes for granted and doesn't bother to say. Obviously, the boundary between semantics and pragmatics is vague, and at the present time various scholars are apt to disagree about where the boundary is. Some of the contents of this chapter may be considered more "pragmatics" than "semantics" by some people.

Pragmatics deals with utterances, by which we mean specific events, the

7 Pragmatics

intentional acts of speakers at times and places, typically involving language.

Pragmatics is the relation between language and its context of use (and the study of this relation). Pragmatics is important in the understanding of how language works, because linguistic form alone fails to explain all the meanings that we readily get from language. For example, when people ask *if we know what time it is*, they wish to know the *time*. What happens is that meanings which are absent in the forms of language may be inferred from the context, given certain principles about how we use language.

In contrast to semantics, pragmatics involves perception augmented by some species of "ampliative" inference—induction, inference to the best explanation, Bayesian reasoning, or perhaps some special application of general principles special to communication, as conceived by Grice (see below)—but in any case, a sort of reasoning that goes beyond the application of rules, and makes inferences beyond what is established by the basic facts about what expressions are used and their meanings.

The facts with which pragmatics deals with are of various sorts, including:

- Facts about the objective facts of the utterance, including who the speaker is, when the utterance occurred, and where;

- Facts about the speaker's intentions, on the near side, what language the speaker intends to be using, what meaning he/she intends to be using, whom he/she intends to refer to with various shared names, whether a pronoun is used demonstratively or anaphorically, and the like, on the far side, what he/she intends to achieve by saying what she does.

- Facts about beliefs of the speaker and those to whom /he/she speaks, and the conversation they are engaged in; what beliefs they share; what is the focus of the conversation; what they are talking about, etc.

- Facts about relevant social institutions, such as promises, marriage ceremonies, courtroom procedures, and the like, which affect what a person accomplishes in or by saying what he/she does.

In the next section, we will focus on five sorts of language which requires pragmatic inference.

7.2 Five Linguistic Situations Requiring Pragmatic Inference

Firstly, we will consider five sorts of meanings which can be inferred by computing language with its context of use: (a) ambiguous words, phrases, and sentences; (b) deictics; (c) figures of speech; (d) indirect illocution, and (e) presupposition.

7.2.1 Ambiguity

Ambiguity exists when a form has two or more meanings. Ambiguity is different from vagueness. With vagueness, the number of possible meanings is quite open. For example, there is vagueness when I say, "*I bought a dog.*" The dog could be male or female, brown or white, big or small, St. Bernard or Chihuahua, etc. But in "*Can you see the [bič]?*" two meanings contrast quite crisply: "*Can you see the beech?*" and "*Can you see the beach?*" Pragmatics, ordinarily, would make clear which meaning is appropriate—in the forest the former and at the seashore the latter.

There are two kinds of ambiguous language: **lexical ambiguity** and **structural ambiguity**.

Lexical Ambiguity

Lexical ambiguity is ambiguity in the form of a morpheme or word. Lexical ambiguity results from the existence of **homonyms**, cases in which a single form has two or more meanings, as in English [tu] (*to, too,* and *two*), and *tear* ([tɪr]) and ([tɛr]). These two examples represent the two sorts of homonyms: **homophones**, like [tu], and **homographs**, like *tear*.

Homophones

A homophone is a single pronunciation with two or more meanings. English examples in addition to [tu] are [flaʊər], which could be either *flower* or *flour*.

Homographs

A homograph is a single spelling with two or more meanings. English examples in addition to *tear* are *read*, which could be either [rid], the present tense form of *read*, or [rɛd] the past tense form of *read*, and *wind, does,* and *use*. Some homographs are also homophones, like *bat* [bæt] "club for hitting in baseball" and "type of flying rodent", and *hide* [haɪd] "skin (noun)" and "conceal (verb)".

Homonymy vs Polysemy

Homonymy may often be distinguished from polysemy. In the last chapter, we've discussed polysemy. Here, we will focus on the difference between polysemy and homonymy. Polysemy occurs when the form of a word suggests different meanings, but the meanings are all related by semantic extension. English examples of polysemy are *drive*, as in "drive animals" and "drive a car", and *wave*, which can be a verb or a noun.

Homonymy and polysemy are not always clearly distinct, because it isn't always apparent whether or not different meanings are related by semantic extension. *Cool* [kul], "low in temperature" and "clam in mind/demeanor", is historically an example of polysemy, but nowadays some might feel that these meanings are so different that it better represents homonymy, like *bat*. *Ear* "listening organ of the body" and *ear* as in "ear of corn" are historically different words which came to be pronounced and spelled with the passage of time, but some may reasonably now consider this a case of polysemy, supposing "ear of corn" to be a metaphoric extension of "ear for listening".

Structural Ambiguity

Structural ambiguity exists when a phrase or sentence has two or more meanings because of structure, either of grouping or function (grammatical relations). Thus, structural ambiguity is also called syntactic ambiguity.

Learning and Research Resources

● 中国知网 CNKI
http://www.cnki.net/

CNKI(China National Knowledge Infrastructure, 中国知网) is a key national research and information publishing institution in China, led by Tsinghua University, and supported by Ministry of Education of the People's Republic of China, Ministry of Science and Techndagy of the People's Republic of China, Publicity Department of the CPC Central Committee Communist Party of China and PRC General Administration of Press and Publication of the

People's Republic of China. CNKI has built a comprehensive China Integrated Knowledge Resources System, including journals, doctoral dissertations, masters' theses, proceedings, newspapers, yearbooks, statistical yearbooks, ebooks, patents, standards and so on.

1. Can you search CNKI for the latest research about "ambiguity?"

7.2.2 Deictics

All languages have deictics. **Deictics** are morphemes with variable referential meanings depending on the context of use. Deictics include pronouns, adverbs that refer to space and time, and definiteness morphemes including the "definite article" *the* in English. If it weren't for pragmatics, which ordinarily makes their reference clear, deictic usage could result in a lot of vagueness. In fact, we are seldom puzzled by deictic usage, even though deictics are among the most frequent words and morphemes of a language.

Personal Deictics

Personal pronouns in English include *I, me, she, your, they*, etc., which may distinguish person, number, gender, and grammatical relation. So *I* may be said to mean "the person speaking (or writing) who is subject of the verb", *you* "the person or persons addressed (subject or object)", and *her* "the female person spoken of who is a possessor or object". But who this person is varies with the particular occasion of use of the pronoun. Of course, there can be vagueness and ambiguity in the use of these or any of the deictics. Notice how we can mean "I and the person (s) spoken to", or "I and some other person(s) not spoken to". These are termed the "inclusive" and "exclusive" senses, respectively, of this pronoun.

Temporal Deictics

These are adverbs which refer to time, like *then, now, today,* and *yesterday. Today* means "this day" when spoken today, "yesterday" when spoken yesterday, "tomorrow" when spoken tomorrow, and June 1, 1647 when spoken on June 1, 1647.

Definiteness

This is communicated in various ways in languages. English communicates definiteness particularly with the definite article *the*, with demonstratives including *this*, and *that*, and with the personal pronouns *my, your, her, his,* etc.

A speaker says, "I went to a wedding" and, later, "The wedding was last Saturday". The second sentence, with *the*, assumes or presupposes the hearer's knowledge of the wedding. When someone says, "Have you heard that song?" that shows that the hearer is assumed to know what song is being referred to. As in interpreting personal, temporal, and spatial deictics, interpreting definiteness requires us to consider the context, particularly the speaker, and the knowledge which we share with the speaker, part of which has been created by conversation that has gone immediately before. Recall that *the* is the most frequent word of English, so it must play a very important role in marking a speaker's understanding of what they consider to be knowledge shared with hearers.

7.2.3 Indirect Illocution

In the terminology of philosopher J. L. Austin (1955), simply to speak is to perform a locution, but to speak with an intent, such as to ask, promise, request, plead, assert, demand, order, apologise, warn, or threaten, is to perform an **illocution**. This purpose, or illocutionary intent, is meaningful and will ordinarily be recognized by hearers (or readers), whether it is directly (overtly) expressed or indirectly (inovertly) expressed.

Direct illocution is making the intent of speech evident in the overt form of sentences. There are two ways to make overt or direct illocutions: by using special grammatical forms which directly express the intent, as in English yes/no questions in which an auxiliary verb precedes the subjects as in *Can I go now?*(vs *You have it on my desk by Monday morning.*); by using a performative verb as in:

(a) I warn you not to do that again.
(b) I promise that I'll be there.
(c) We request a booth in the back.

Indirect illocution is leaving the intent of speech unexpressed in the form of sentences. Consider the example of the common English question *Do you know what time it is?* This has the form of a yes/no question, but everybody understands it to be an information question. An appropriate answer to this question is not "Yes" or "No", but a time, like "Two twenty-five", or "A quarter to eight". The sentence is directly a yes/no question, but indirectly it is an information question, and, by pragmatic inference, almost everyone understands it so.

There is usually no special grammatical form for an illocution, though in some languages there are more grammatical markers of illocutions than those in English. Here are some examples of indirect illocution:

Don't do that again.—an indirect warning
I'll be there.—an indirect promise
A booth at the window would be nice.—an indirect request
OK, team, let's get started.—an indirect command

Like ambiguities, deictics, and figures of speech, indirect illocutions are very common, and they are readily recognized by hearers/readers, who interpret them by pragmatic inference.

7.2.4 Figure of Speech

It is common, if not always easy, to distinguish literal and non-literal or figurative language. We usually take certain meanings to be basic, expected, or literal language. Figurative, or non-literal language is novel and creative, and suggests other meanings, like *Drop me a line, Give me a break*, and *Get a life in English*. Non-literal language is frequent and part of everyone's ordinary speech, but by pragmatic inference hearers/readers ordinarily recognize non-literal language, and readily make reasonable inferences about its meaning.

The different types of such creative language use are termed "figures of speech". Six commonly encountered figures of speech are metaphor, metonymy, synecdoche, personification, hyperbole, and irony.

Group-Work Activities

The functions of metaphors in Chinese poetry and in Western poetry are the same, though the vehicles and tenors in them may be different thanks to the different climates, natural environments, lifestyles and cultures of the peoples.

1. Can you find any metaphors that appear both in Chinese and English poems?

2. Read the following piece of poem and analyse the metaphors in it.

青山横北郭, *Blue mountains to the north of the walls,*
白水绕东城。*White river winding about them.*
此地一为别, *Here we must make separation,*
孤蓬万里征。*And go out through a thousand miles of dead grass.*
浮云游子意, *Mind like a floating wide cloud,*
落日故人情。*Sunset like the parting of old acquaintances.*
挥手自兹去, *Who bow over their clasped hands at a distance,*
萧萧班马鸣。*Our horses neigh to each other as we are departing.*

If you desire to know more about metaphors and metonymies in classical Chinese poetry, please visit this website: https://www.translationjournal.net/July-2015/metaphors-and-metonymies-in-classical-chinese-poetry-and-their-english-translations.html

Synecdoche

This is using a part to mean the whole, a type of metaphor or metonymy: "Can I borrow your wheels? (wheels = cars)"; "There is still great respect for the crown. (crown = monarchy)"

The latter example is a type of metonymy if crown is not part of meaning of monarchy, but just an association with it.

Personification

This is a type of metaphor in which human characteristics are attributed to something non-human, which shows similar characteristics: "This drawer refuses to open (refuses to open = is stuck)" ; "My goldfish is begging to be fed (is begging to be fed = looks very hungry)."

Hyperbole

This is a type of metaphor in which comparison is implied to a similar but extravagant case: "Drop dead!" ; "I'd rather kill myself than watch music videos."

Irony

This is a type of metaphor in which comparison is implied to an opposite or unreasonable extreme case: "That's cute! (Said of something not cute at all)"; "Let's keep the noise down to an uproar, please. (When the noise is not at "uproar" level)"

7.2.5 Presupposition

A presupposition is something assumed (presupposed) to be true in a sentence which asserts other information, for example, sentence (a1) presupposes (a2), (b1) presupposes (b2), and (c1) presupposes (c2).

(a1) *Christopher realized that Winnie was gone.*
(a2) *Winnie was gone.*

(b1) *Christopher stopped looking.*
(b2) *Christopher had been looking.*

(c1) *The owl sneezed again.*
(c2) *The owl had sneezed before.*

The information of second sentences is presupposed, rather than entailed or included some way in the first. It is apparent in the fact that if the first sentence is negated the truth of the second sentence is unchanged: (e), (f), and (g) also presuppose (a2), (b2), and (c2), respectively.

(e) *Christopher didn't realize that Winne was gone.*
(f) *Christopher didn't stop looking.*
(g) *The owl didn't sneeze again.*

In presupposition, furthermore, if the second sentence is false the first is false or unreasonable. Thus, the respective truth of (h), (i), and (j) makes (a1), (a2), and (b2) false or unreasonable.

(h) *Winnie wasn't gone.* (So, Christopher could not have realized that he was gone.)

(i) *Christopher had not been looking.* (So, he could not have stopped looking.)

(j) *The owl hadn't sneezed before.* (So, it could not have sneezed again.)

Group-Work Activities

According to Mencius, education must awaken the innate abilities of the human mind. He advocated active interrogation of the text, saying, "One who believes all of a book would be better off without books". (尽信书,不如无书。)

1. What is the presupposition in this sentence?
2. How do you understand this sentence?
3. Do you agree with Mencius's idea?

Presupposition vs Synonymy and Entailment

Think about what we've learned in the last chapter about synonymy and entailment. How do we distinguish *presupposition, synonymy* and *entailment*? It is helpful to distinguish presupposition from **synonym** and **entailment**. **Synonymy** is the relationship between paraphrases, such as (k1) and (k2), and (m1) and (m2).

(k1) *Kanga give Piglet a bath.*
(k2) *Kanga bathed Piglet.*

(m1) *Pooh was too short to reach the honey.*
(m2) *Pooh wasn't tall enough to reach the honey.*

If either of two synonymous sentences is true so is the other, and if either is false so is the other.

Entailment is the relationship of logical inclusion between the circumstances described by pairs of sentences, as where (n1) entails (n2), and (o1) entails (o2).

(n1) *Christopher has a bear and a pig.*
(n2) *Christopher has a bear.*

(o1) *Christopher dropped Winnie.*
(o2) *Winnie fell.*

In these relationships, if the first sentence is false the second could be either true or false, and if the second sentence is false so is the first. Thus, if Christopher doesn't have a bear and a pig he might or might not have a bear (or a pig, though not both), but if he doesn't have a bear, then he certainly doesn't have a bear and a pig. Likewise, if Christopher didn't drop Winnie, then Winnie may still have fallen, some way, but if in fact Winnie didn't fall, then it cannot be the case that Christopher or anyone else dropped him.

These understandings result because an entailed sentence describes a broader or more inclusive circumstance than an entailing sentence. In these examples, having a bear is a circumstance which includes having a bear and a pig, and falling may result from a number of circumstances besides being dropped.

7.3 Speech Act Theory

Before we delve more deeply into utterance meaning, let's return briefly to syntax. We use certain kinds of syntactic structures, called *sentence types*, when speaking interrogatives (questions), imperatives (commands), and declaratives (statements).

Is it raining? (interrogative)
Get out! (command)
I'd like a sandwich. (statement)

In pragmatic terms (recall the train example), each utterance we make carries communicative force and can be thought of as performing a particular act, what we call a **speech act**. If you were to say, "Is it raining?" you would have performed a speech act. When sentence type corresponds with our intention, it is a **direct speech act**. The speech act *Is it raining* is a direct speech act if uttered with the intention of asking a question about the truth or falsity of the current level of precipitation. Direct speech acts are the sum of the meanings of their parts. You typically ask a question when you don't know something, and you ask someone so you can have an answer, for example, "Can you juggle?" The appropriate answer would be either *yes* or *no*. In a direct speech act, the intention and effect are predictable; a question is a request for information to which a particular reply is appropriate. Now, what about this sentence: "Have you cleaned your room yet?" This sentence is also an interrogative in terms of sentence type, but does it have to be a question? Not necessarily. What if you have asked your daughter repeatedly to clean her room and told her that if she doesn't, she won't be allowed to go the movies as planned? Uttering this interrogative sentence type actually conveys a (mild) threat: If you don't clean your room, then no movies for you! This sentence (which we'll also assume is an utterance) is an **indirect speech act**: its meaning depends on context rather than on sentence type.

This is just a simple illustration of the complexity of speech acts and of how sentence type does not always correspond to speaker intention (nor, for that matter, to hearer interpretation). **Speech act theory** tries to explain more precisely how meaning and action are related to language. Speech act theory (originally introduced by Austin in 1962) is concerned with the communicative intentions of speakers and how they achieve their communicative goals. John Austin proposes that communication is a series of communicative acts that are used systematically to accomplish particular purposes and that all utterances perform actions by having a specific force assigned to them. Austin offers three basic kinds of acts that are simultaneously performed by an utterance. They can be informally described as follows:

locutionary act: an utterance with a particular sense and reference (closest to meaning in the traditional sense, the sum of its parts);

illocutionary act: the act (defined by social convention) that is performed by making the utterance: a statement, offer, promise, bet, etc.;

perlocutionary act: the effects on the audience, whether intended or unintended, brought about by the utterance.

Examples are useful here. Suppose a teacher says, "Jo, would you like to read your poem first?" The locutionary speech act is the literal meaning of the question, namely, whether Jo is interested in reading her poem. The illocutionary speech act is, by social convention, a request that Jo read her poem. The perlocutionary act is its effect on Jo, who might agree or refuse to read her poem.

Although speech act theorists have proposed these three general types of speech acts, they are primarily interested in speaker intentions: the illocutionary force of utterances. To study this facet of human communication, various types of speech acts have been proposed. Below are five described in Searle's (1979) seminal book on speech acts: (a) Assertives/Representatives; (b) Directives; (c) Commissive; (d) Declarations; (e) Expressive.

Assertives/Representatives
Utterances reporting statements of fact verifiable as true or false (e.g. *I am old enough to vote; Columbus discovered American in 1492; Water freezes at zero degrees centigrade*.).

Directives
Utterances intended to get someone to do something (e.g. *Stop shouting; Take out the garbage.*).

Commissive
Utterances committing one to doing something (e.g. *I promise to call you later; I'll write your letter of recommendation tomorrow.*).

Declarations
Utterances bringing about a change in the state of affairs (e.g. *I now pronounce you husband and wife; I hereby sentence you to ten years in jail.*).

Expressive
Utterances expressing speaker attitudes (e.g. *That"s a beautiful dress; I'm sorry for being so late.*).

7.4 Cooperative Talk: Conversational Rules

As speakers, we also share certain implicit conversational rules for how to communicate spoken and unspoken messages. These conversational rules are crucial for successful communication, and we are well aware of how to follow them, or in some cases how to ignore them, in order to convey a particular message. We'll also see that these rules of conversation can vary across languages and cultures, and the lack of shared knowledge regarding these rules can lead to communication breakdown.

The philosopher Paul Grice proposed the following **maxims of conversation**, which continue to be an accurate description of the shared rules that speakers use in interactions.

Maxim of Quantity

(a) Make your contribution to the conversation as informative as necessary.

(b) Do not make your contribution to the conversation more informative than necessary.

All communicants must strike a balance between providing too much and too little information when they speak or write. In the example below, both speakers achieve this balance because they directly answer each of the questions they are asked.

A: *Have any of the supervisors been in?*
B: *Oh yeah, I've had a lot of visitors lately, um… I went downstairs to get something to eat and somebody was waiting at the door today.*
A: *Who was it?*
B: *John Wood. Do you know him?*
A: *No.*
B: *He was um…*
A: *Is he an old guy?*
B: *No kind of a young guy.*

Speaker B, for instance, directly answers A's question about whether any supervisors had come in. B provides slightly more information than necessary, saying that many visitors had come in, but this extra information does not exceed the amount of detail that would be provided in a conversation of this nature.

Maxim of Quality
(a) Do not say what you believe to be false.
(b) Do not say that for which you lack adequate evidence.

When we communicate, there is a tacit assumption that what each communicant says or writes will be truthful. For instance, when speaker A below asks B who she is going to spend the evening with, A expects B to give a truthful answer.

A: *So who are you going out with tonight?*
B: *Koosh and Laura.*

This may seem like a fairly obvious point, but conversational implicatures definitely result when an utterance is judged as not being truthful. The excerpt below was taken from the first page of a marketing survey enclosed with a child's toy:

Please take a moment to let us know something about yourself. Your valuable input enables us to continue to develop our advanced learning tools.

Following this statement were a series of questions eliciting information not just about the quality of the toy but about the occupations of household members, their annual income, the kinds of automobiles they drove, and so forth. In this context, many people will interpret the above statement as less than truthful: the manufacturer is not solely interested in improving its "advanced learning tools." Instead, it wants to gather demographic information about the parents who purchased the toy so that they can be targeted in the future with advertisements for other toys.

7 Pragmatics

Even though communicants place great faith in the truth of the assertions that they make and hear, there are certain situations when violating the Quality Maxim is considered acceptable. For instance, if someone asks you "Do you like my new hairstyle?" it would be highly inappropriate in most contexts to reply "No," since this could result in hurt feelings. Therefore, in most communicative contexts, many people would reply "Yes" or "It"s great" even if their replies are untruthful. Of course, the person to whom the reply is directed would undoubtedly judge the reply as truthful. But as will be noted in a later section, politeness is such an important pragmatic concept in English that it overrides other pragmatic considerations.

Maxim of Relevance
(a) Say only things that are relevant.

The notion of what is relevant in discourse will vary from one context to another. For instance, in the conversation below, speaker B asks A if he started his new job. However, a few turns later, B changes the topic entirely, cutting off any further discussion of A's job and shifting the topic to a phone call B had received the previous night:

B: *Are you um... how's your new job? Did you start?*
A: *I just was painting and I do a little carpentry a little gutter work and stuff.*
B: *Uh huh.*
A: *So I've been doing that.*
B: *Someone called for you last night.*
A: *Really?*
B: *Yeah.*
A: *Who was it?*
B: *But I told him you were you weren't working here anymore.*

In casual conversation, such topic shifts are normal, since there are no real pre-planned topics that people intend to discuss when they converse casually, and in many instances they are free to change topics, digress, etc., without violating the maxim of relation.

Maxim of Manner
(a) Avoid obscurity of expression.
(b) Avoid ambiguity.
(c) Be brief (avoid unnecessary wordiness).
(d) Be orderly.

Clarity of expression is highly valued in what we say and write. For instance, someone going to a public forum on global warming expects his/her information on this potentially technical topic to be understandable to a general audience, not scientists already quite familiar with the subject. This is why the excerpt below on this topic contains so much metadiscourse, such as "*My talk will be split into four sections*," that comment directly on how a particular piece of discourse is being organized (other examples of metadiscourse are in boldface):

But **what I'd like to talk to you about** uh this afternoon just uh briefly because we only have forty-five minutes is uh studying climate change from space. And **my talk will split into four uhm sections**. I'll spend a **few minutes talking about the climate system** and uh then having sort of looked at that we'll ask the question and hopefully answer it uh why observe from space. There are many parts of the climate system that we could discuss uhm but uh **I thought I would concentrate on** polar ice, and any of you who saw ITV's *News at Ten* last night uh will have a foretaste of at least one of the things that I uh will address. And then **I'll say a few words about** where do we go next, uh what's going to happen in the future. **So we'll start with** what is the climate system.

The speaker so explicitly tells her audience what she will discuss because she knows that the people to whom she is speaking do not have a written text at hand to refer to, and she wants to provide them with a global framework of her talk so that they will be able to anticipate what she will be discussing.

The conversational maxims go hand in hand with Grice's **cooperative principle**, another principle of conversation, which assumes that the participants in a conversation will make a conversational contribution such as is required, at the stage at which it occurs, by the accepted purpose or direction of the talk exchange. At its core, the cooperative principle means that in conversation, we don't lie, nor do we assume our conversational partners lie—we are sincere, and for the most part, we contribute relevant information. Grice recognized the difference between sentence meaning and speaker intention (similar to direct and indirect speech acts). He proposed that speakers assume that the hearer can interpret additional meaning based on the context or communicative situation and does not rely on the meanings of the words alone. Grice refers to this kind of meaning as **speaker meaning**.

Group-Work Activities

● *Cao Cao went to inquire his future of a wise man of Runan named Xu Shao.*

"What manner of man am I?" asked Cao Cao.

The seer made no reply, and again and again Cao Cao pressed the question.

Then Xu Shao replied, "In peace you are an able subject; in chaos you are a crafty hero!" Cao Cao greatly rejoiced to hear this.

Please discuss the following questions:
1. Does Xu Shao's answer obey the maxim of manner?
2. Why did Cao greatly rejoice to hear it?
3. What's your comment on Xu Shao's answer?

The importance of manner is emphasized in Chinese traditional literature. Here are some examples.

子曰:"知及之,仁不能守之,虽得之,必失之;知及之,仁能守之,不庄以莅之,则民不敬;知及之,仁能守之,庄以莅之,动之不以礼,未善也。"

——《论语·卫灵公》

君子不失色于人,不失口于人。

——《礼记》

语言学入门 *Essentials for Classical General Linguistics*

> 人无礼，而不生；事无礼，而不成；国无礼，而不宁。
>
> ——《荀子》
>
> 1. How do you interpret the importance of manner proclaimed in these excerpts?
> 2. Can you find more examples in Chinese classic literature about the importance of manner in speech?

7.5 Syntax vs Semantics vs Pragmatics

Clause type system may raise vexing issues concerning the interrelationship between syntax and semantics/pragmatics. Consider the relationship between the declarative clause *Tina is sensible* and the interrogative *Is Tina sensible* Semantically, they are partly alike and partly different. What they share is a common propositional meaning: both express the proposition "Tina is sensible." Where they differ most is in their non-propositional meaning, more specifically in their illocutionary force: a typical utterance of the declarative would be a statement used to assert the proposition, but a typical utterance of the interrogative would be a question used to question the proposition. Statements, questions, and directives are in essence pragmatic categories. Each represents a very general class of speech acts which embraces a range of more specific categories: e.g. assertions and predictions as types of statement; orders, requests and invitations as types of directive (see Huddleston and Pullum 2002, p.858; Quirk et al. 1985, p. 804). Beyond these there are a vast number of illocutionary categories that are not subsumed under any of the general categories, such as promises, congratulations, bets, wishes, and the like.

While clause type is an important determinant of illocutionary force, it is not the only one. For instance, if a declarative such as *Maria is Spanish* is uttered with rising intonation, it will typically turn into a question which would otherwise be a statement. One special device of relevance here is the *performative* use of verbs that denote illocutionary acts (e.g. *admit, swear, urge, apologize, warn, suggest*), which may affect the performance of the very acts they denote. Performative utterances are characterized by a precise specification of illocutionary force, which is identified in their propositional content (thus the warning force of *I warn you to leave* is identifiable in the proposition it expresses, but the statement force of *I warned you to leave.* is not similarly identified in its propositional content).

Unlike the syntactic categories of clause type, illocutionary categories are not mutually exclusive. Where an utterance has more than one illocutionary force, as Huddleston and Pullum (2002, p. 859) observe, one will be primary or salient and the other secondary. For example, in a typical utterance of *I advise you to make an appointment* the advice force is primary and the statement force secondary (the statement is simply the means by which the advice is issued, as reflected in the greater likelihood that the utterance would be reported as *You advised me to make an appointment.* rather than *You said you advised me to make an appointment*).

When the illocutionary force of an utterance is different from that normally conveyed by the clause type concerned, we have what is generally referred to as an *indirect speech act,* for example, a typical utterance of the imperative clause *Have a nice holiday* will have the (indirect) force of a wish rather than a directive, insofar as having a nice holiday is not normally considered to be within the addressee's control; similarly, the closed interrogative *Do you have a cigarette* is often used as an indirect request for a cigarette, and in this case the question about the addressee's possession of a cigarette is of secondary importance to the indirect request. Indirect speech acts have varying degrees of indirectness. Compare for instance a mother's *It's getting late* uttered with the intention of directing her child to go to bed, where there is a considerable discrepancy between the indirect directive meaning "Go to bed" and the proposition directly expressed by the declarative "It is getting late" with a job applicant's *I wish to apply for the position advertised*, where the applicant will be readily understood to have performed the illocutionary act of applying for the position in question, rather than merely wishing to do so, insofar as the wish is satisfied simply by the submission of the application.

Indirect illocutionary force may be signalled in various ways. For instance, the exclamatory statement force of the interrogative *Gee, is he strong* is reinforced by the non-propositional marker *gee* and by the likely selection of a falling intonation terminal, rather than the rising terminal typically associated with closed questions. Often used as an indicator of indirect illocutionary force is the conventional use of certain expressions, for example. the use of the modal *can* and the adverb *please* in a request such as *Can you pass the salt, please*, where by contrast *Are you able to pass the salt* is unlikely (unless there is actual doubt as to the addressee's ability to perform the desired activity).

Learning and Research Resources

● 知网研学

https://x.cnki.net/search/home

This is a tool to insert in-text citations while simultaneously creating a bibliography, which helps you organize references automatically as you work. It can be linked with CNKI, so you can easily insert many research papers in your own writing.

● 维普期刊

http://qikan.cqvip.com/

维普期刊 covers many academic journal articles in different areas, so you can find many Chinese articles here. Besides, it provides an academic writing check system and other services. Now, try to search this website for some latest articles about the speech act.

Summary

Social communication (pragmatics) is not simply the product of decoding the words in a sentence or utterance and then determining their meaning. Pragmatics studies language that is not directly spoken, where the speaker hints or suggests a meaning, and the listener assumes the correct intention. In a sense, pragmatics is seen as an understanding between people to obey certain rules of interaction. For example, every parent know that when a child utters *Dad, I'm still hungry after finishing a snack*, the child is not simply making a declarative statement: he is requesting more food. The parent reaches this conclusion on the basis of information derived from the social context itself, not simply the individual words of the utterance. And to correctly interpret the meaning of this utterance, the parent has to understand the illocutionary force of the child's utterance: the child's intentions in uttering the sentence. In determining that the child is issuing a directive, the parent draws upon a number of contextual clues, particularly the fact that he has heard this very same utterance on many occasions after his child has completed a snack.

> ## Learning Highlights: Read and Think—Linguistics and Life
>
> *Pragmatic language is a complex, multi-faceted domain that includes such diverse skill sets as reciprocal conversational skills (e.g. turn-taking), word choice based on specific conversational partners (e.g. register), and the comprehension and use of non-verbal aspects of communication that complement speech... Pragmatic language is often studied by eliciting structured discourse through conversation or narrative. Conversation and narrative both involve a complex suite of processes: linguistic (e.g. syntax), cognitive (e.g. story organization), and social (e.g. maintaining listener interest).*
>
> 1. How do you understand the three processes pragmatics involves?
> 2. Can you give one example of conversation to illustrate the use of diverse skills for certain pragmatic effect?
>
> *One of the basic problems which is legitimately proposed as a primary candidate for neuropragmatic research is the nature and neuro-cognitive representation of literal meaning... Linguistics has strived to pin down the essentials of literal meanings as a means, among other things, to keep semantics and pragmatics distinct. In a survey of the literature, Ariel (2002) found it impossible to identify one agreed upon criterion for "literal meaning" as a theoretical construct. Indeed, it seems that there are arguments against the necessity of each of the properties mentioned above, and pragmatics on one side, cognitive semantics on the other side, have done much to demonstrate that (a) there is much nonliterality in presumed literal meanings and (b) non-literal meanings share many of the properties which are generally attributed to literal meanings.*
>
> 1. How do you understand the relationship between literal meaning and nonliteral meaning?
> 2. Can you interpret the literal and nonliteral meaning of the following

words?

| 朕 孤 臣妾 草民 鄙人 哀家 本宫 老夫 小生 贫僧 贫道 贫尼 本仙君 洒家 不才 |

Research Fronts

• Carl S. Blyth and Julie M. Sykes did a research about how modern technology enhanced pragmatics teaching in specific contexts.

... *As a well-known researcher in L2 pragmatics, Gabriele Kasper recognized that interlanguage pragmatics research needed to include studies of classroom-based instruction and assessment. Fortunately, scholars interested in L2 learning and teaching heeded Kasper's call and began to examine the effects of instruction on the learning of pragmalinguistic forms and sociocultural norms. For example, recent L2 pragmatics textbooks such as Ishihara & Cohen (2010), McConachy (2017) and Cohen (2018), and journal articles such as Gironzetti & Koike (2016) and Taguchi (2015), as well as monographs based on empirical studies such as van Compernolle (2014) have shed light on the role of instruction in the development of L2 pragmatic competence...*

They investigated the efficacy of using computer-assisted video to teach the English pragmatics to international students:

... *Noting that there are few studies that examine the effects of different types of input and feedback on the production of extended oral discourse, the authors developed computerized video simulations of requesting behaviour that required students to produce oral responses to specific prompts in English-language scenarios. To test the effects of implicit vs explicit instruction, the authors devised two different conditions within the computerized simulations. In the implicit condition, a cohort of students watched videos of unscripted role plays of a low imposition request and a high imposition request. The videos contained no metapragmatic explanation....In addition, students in the explicit condition were asked to complete brief exercises on paper to solidify their understanding of the explicit instruction. Finally, both groups were asked to*

7 Pragmatics

> *report what pragmatic knowledge they had obtained from the input...*
>
> They also suggested the future directions of research on instructional pragmatics:
>
> *... We anticipate this to be especially relevant in light of the Covid-19 pandemic that has forced educators to move their in-person classes to online formats. While the long-term educational effects of the sudden move to online instruction remain to be seen, there is little doubt that technology will continue to play an important role in L2 instruction...*

Self-Study Activities

1. What are the rules that guide the speaker and hearer to make pragmatic inference? Can you illustrate the process with one example?

2. Match the construction in the left-hand column with the speech act with which it is associated in the right-hand column.

   (1) The English language originated in England   a. Assertive/Representative
   (2) I promise to do the work   b. Directive
   (3) I hereby declare the meeting open   c. Commissive
   (4) Don't take too long   d. Declaration
   (5) I'm sorry I broke the glass   e. Expressive

3. Imagine a context in which one will say *I wouldn't mind another glass of wine.* What are its grammatical meaning and pragmatic meaning?

4. Which expressions in the conversation below are grammatically well-formed sentences? Explain your choices.

   Speaker A: I really like chocolate ice cream.
   Speaker B: Me too. My second favourite flavour is vanilla.
   Speaker A: I don't care for vanilla. Too tasteless, in my opinion.
   Speaker B: Really? I think it has great taste.

5. Discuss whether the speech acts listed below is direct or indirect.

   (1) A teacher says to her students: "Please leave your papers on my desk."
   (2) One person says to another sitting next to an open door leading to the

backyard of a house: "Lots of mosquitoes are getting into the house."

(3) A son says to his mother: "I'll take out the garbage later."

(4) A guest at a dinner party says to another guest during dinner, "Could you please pass the butter?"

6. Two speakers (Fred and Hazel) are gossiping about a third person (Christine). Fred says: "Christine is always late for work. I think she's going to get fired. She's a totally irresponsible worker." Noticing that Christine is approaching and that Fred doesn't realize this, Hazel asks Fred, "Do you think it will rain later today?"

(1) Which of the maxims of the cooperative principle (quantity, relation, manner, and quality) has Hazel violated?

(2) What is the conversational implicature of this violation?

7. What makes good writing? Do Grice's maxims of the cooperative principle also apply to writing?

8. Why are younger speakers more likely to use slang than older speakers?

9. The following words all mean "I" (我). Could you please think about when we use them or how they are used in different contexts? Do their usages connect with different identities?

朕 孤 臣妾 草民 鄙人 哀家 本宫 老夫 小生 贫僧 贫道 贫尼 本仙君 洒家 不才

Further Reading

See J. L. Austin's *How to Do Things with Words* (Oxford University Press, 1962) for an early discussion of the notion of pragmatic vs grammatical meaning.

A description of speech act theory can be found in J. Searle's *Expression and Meaning* (Cambridge University Press, 1979).

The cooperative principle is outlined in H. P. Grice's *Studies in the Way of Words* (Cambridge, MA: Harvard University Press, 1989).

For a general overview of the field of pragmatics, see S. Levinson's *Pragmatics* (Cambridge University Press, 1983).

7 Pragmatics

Outline

I. Pragmatics is another branch of linguistics that is concerned with meaning.
   A. Pragmatics and semantics can be viewed as different parts, or different aspects, of the same general study.
   B. Both are concerned with people's ability to use language meaningfully.
   C. Semantics is mainly concerned with a speaker's competence to use the language system in producing meaningful utterances and processing (comprehending) utterances produced by others.
   D. The chief focus of pragmatics is a person's ability to derive meanings from specific kinds of speech situations:
       i) to recognize what the speaker is referring to
       ii) to relate new information to what has gone before
       iii) to interpret what is said from background knowledge about the speaker and the topic of discourse
       iv) to infer or "fill in" information that the speaker takes for granted and doesn't bother to say
II. Pragmatics deals with *utterances*, by which we will mean specific events, the intentional acts of speakers at times and places, typically involving language.
III. There are five sorts of meanings which can be inferred by computing language from its context of use: (1) ambiguous words, phrases, and sentences, (2) deictics, (3) figures of speech, (4) indirect illocution, and (5) presupposition.
IV. **Ambiguity** exists when a form has two or more meanings. Pragmatics, ordinarily, would make clear which meaning is appropriate. There are two kinds of ambiguous language: **lexical ambiguity** and **structural ambiguity**.
   A. Lexical ambiguity is ambiguity in the form of a morpheme or word.
   B. Structural ambiguity exists when a phrase or sentence has two or more meanings because of structure, either grouping or function (grammatical relations).
V. **Direct illocution** is making the intent of speech evident in the overt form of sentences.
VI. **Indirect illocution** is leaving the intent of speech unexpressed or unovert in the form of sentences.
VII. There are six commonly encountered figures of speech, which are metaphor,

metonymy, synecdoche, personification, hyperbole, and irony.

A. **Synecdoche** is using a part to mean the whole, a type of metaphor or metonymy.

B. **Hyperbole** is another type of metaphor in which comparison is implied to a similar but extravagant case.

C. **Irony** is a type of metaphor in which comparison is implied to an opposite or unreasonable extreme case.

VIII. A presupposition is something assumed (presupposed) to be true in a sentence which asserts other information.

A. Entailment is different from preposition because it is the relationship of logical inclusion between the circumstances described by pairs of sentences

IX. Speech **act theory** tries to explain more precisely how meaning and action are related to language. Speech act theory is concerned with the communicative intentions of speakers and how they achieve their communicative goals.

A. *locutionary act*: an utterance with a particular sense and reference (closest to meaning in the traditional sense, the sum of its parts)

B. *illocutionary act*: the act (defined by social convention) that is performed by making the utterance: a statement, offer, promise, bet, etc.

C. *perlocutionary act*: the effects (not necessarily intentional) on the audience, whether intended or unintended, brought about by the utterance

X. There are various types of speech acts that have been proposed.

A. **Assertives/Representatives**: utterances reporting statements of fact verifiable as true or false

B. **Directives**: utterances intended to get someone to do something

C. **Commissives**: utterances committing one to doing something

D. **Declarations**: utterances bringing about a change in the state of affairs

E. **Expressives**: utterances expressing speaker attitudes

Conversational rules are crucial for successful communication, and we are well aware of how to follow them, or in some cases how to ignore them, in order to convey a particular message.

A. Maxim of quantity

B. Maxim of quality

C. Maxim of relevance

D. Maxim of Manner

Glossary

Here we recommend a very useful learning website to all learners. ***The SIL Glossary of Linguistic Terms*** provides information in the form of glossaries and bibliographies designed to support fieldwork and linguistic research (*https://glossary.sil.org/term*).

In the following section, we concluded some terms that appeared in this book, and their definitions are borrowed from different sources.

acoustic phonetics: Acoustic phonetics is a technical area of linguistics. Phoneticians depict and analyse sound waves using machines and computer programs. Acoustic phonetics is the study of sound waves made by the human vocal organs for communication.

adjacency pair: An adjacency pair is a unit of conversation that contains an exchange of one turn each by two speakers. The turns are functionally related to each other in such a fashion that the first turn requires a certain type or range of types of second turn.

adjective phrase: A phrase such as very delicious whose head is an adjective.

adverbial: In linguistics, an adverbial phrase (AdvP) is a multi-word expression operating adverbially: its syntactic function is to modify other expressions, including verbs, adjectives, adverbs, adverbials, and sentences. Adverbial phrases can be divided into two types: complement adverbs and modifier adverbs.

affixation: Affixation is the morphological process. The process of adding derivational suffixes and prefixes to a word (e.g. adding un- and -ness to happy to create unhappiness)

affixes: Prefixes and suffixes added to words. An affix can be a derivational morpheme or an inflectional morpheme.

affricate: A manner of articulation associated with sounds, such as /tʃ/ beginning church, whose articulation is the combination of a plosive and a fricative.

agent: A grammatical agent is the thematic relation of the cause or initiator to an event. The agent is a semantic concept distinct from the subject of a sentence as well as from the topic.

airstream mechanism: The way in which air is made to flow into or out of the vocal tract in order to make a speech sound. There are three major airstream mechanisms: pulmonic, velaric, glottalic.

allomorphs: An allomorph is one of two or more complementary morphs which manifest a morpheme in its different phonological or morphological environments. For instance, the plural morpheme in English is /s/ following nouns ending in an unvoiced sound (e.g. cats) and /z/ following a voiced sound (e.g. dogs).

allophones: Predictable variations in the pronunciation of phonemes. [p] and [pʰ] are allophones of the phoneme /p/. [t] and [tʰ] are allophones of the phoneme /t/.

alveolar ridge: The part of the upper surface of the mouth immediately behind the front teeth.

alveolar: An articulation involving the tip or blade of the tongue and the alveolar ridge, as in English [d] in *die*.

alveolo-palatal: Post-alveolar consonant produced with significant raising of the front of the tongue toward the palate.

antonymy: A relation between words such as happy and unhappy that have opposite meanings.

approximants: A manner of articulation associated with sounds such as

/w/ in which the airstream in the oral cavity flows freely.

article: An article is a member of a small class of determiners that identify a noun's definite or indefinite reference, and new or given status.

articulation: The approach or contact of two speech organs, such as the tip of the tongue and the upper teeth.

articulator: One of several parts of the vocal tract that can be used to form speech sounds.

aspirated/aspiration: A sound, such as /t/ in tack, whose articulation involves a puff of air leaving the mouth.

aspiration: A period of voicelessness after the release of an articulation, as in English in pie [p^haI].

assimilation: Sounds becoming closer in their pronunciation because of their proximity. For instance, when any vowel occurs before a nasal consonant, such as /n/ in man, the vowel will become nasalized too.

auxiliary verbs: An auxiliary verb is a verb which accompanies the lexical verb of a verb phrase, and expresses grammatical distinctions not carried by the lexical verb, such as *person, number, tense, aspect*, and *voice*.

back (of the togue): The part of the tongue below the soft palate.

back vowel: Vowel in which the body of the tongue is in the back part of the oral cavity (mouth). The vowels [ɔ, u, o, ɑ] form a set of back reference vowels.

base form of verb: The form of the verb to which no verb inflections have been added and which can be preceded by the infinitive marker to: to walk, to hit, or to hike.

base: A free morpheme to which affixes can be potentially added. In the word dislikeable, the base is like.

bilabial: An articulation involving both lips, as in English [m] in my.

borrowings: Words that have entered a language from another language.

English has many words from Greek (e.g. telephone) and Latin (e.g. gymnasium). Compare with cognate vocabulary.

bound morpheme: A bound morpheme is a grammatical unit that never occurs by itself, but is always attached to some other morpheme.

broad transcription: A phonetic transcription that captures only phonemic contrasts in words. Compare with narrow transcription.

clause function: Functions such as subject, predicator, and object that indicate relationships between elements in a clause. The noun phrase the car is subject in *The car is broken* but object in *I drove the car*.

clause: A syntactic unit that can be analysed into clause functions. For instance, *The car is old* is a clause because it contains a subject, *the car*; a predicator, *is*; and a subject complement, *old*.

cleft sentence: A cleft sentence is a complex sentence in which a simple sentence is expressed using a main clause and a subordinate clause. In English the prototypical cleft sentence has the following form: *it* + be + X + subordinate clause. X can be a constituent of one of many varieties.

closed class: A closed class is a grammatical class of words with limited membership. These words have primarily grammatical meaning. (e.g. articles, prepositions, auxiliary verbs)

closed syllable: A syllable ending in a consonant, as in run and the two syllables in *mis. fit*.

co-hyponyms: A group of words, such as chair, bed, dresser, and couch, that are each hyponyms of a more general word, in this case furniture.

coda: The coda (also known as auslaut) comprises the consonant sounds of a syllable that follow the nucleus.

cognate vocabulary: Vocabulary that languages share having a common origin in an ancestral language. For instance, words for father in languages such as Spanish (padre), French (père), and German (Vater) are all cognates because they originated in a common ancestral language.

Glossary

coherence: A text that is meaningful and that makes "sense." The two sentences *It was sunny and warm today. Therefore, I wore a winter coat* do not form a coherent sequence because wearing a winter coat is not a logical consequence of the weather being sunny and warm. A more coherent alternative would be *Therefore, I wore a short-sleeve shirt*. Compare with cohesion.

cohesion: Achieved in a text containing explicit markers indicating relationships between various parts of the text. In the sentences *My brother is a doctor. He works at a nearby hospital* the pronoun He in the second sentence creates a cohesive link with the first sentence because it refers back to My brother in the first sentence.

collocations: Words that commonly occur together. For instance, the sentence *I strongly agree* contains two words, *strongly* and *agree*, that commonly co-occur in this context. Other words could certainly follow *strongly*, but are much less likely to do so than *agree* and other words expressing opinions, such as *disagree* or *dislike*.

commissive: A speech act that commits one to doing something: *I promise to send you my latest novel* or *I will make dinner at 5:00*.

complement: In grammar, a complement is a word, phrase, or clause that is necessary to complete the meaning of a given expression. Complements are often also arguments (expressions that help complete the meaning of a predicate).

complex sentence: A complex sentence is a sentence which includes at least one main clause, and at least one subordinate clause.

compound sentence: A compound sentence is a sentence composed of two or more coordinate clauses.

compounding: A compound is a word containing a stem that is made up of more than one root. The meaning of a compound is not simply the sum of the meanings of the two morphemes upon which the compound is based.

conjunction: A conjunction is a word that syntactically links words or larger constituents, and expresses a semantic relationship between them. A conjunction is positionally fixed relative to one or more of the elements related by it, thus distinguishing it from constituents such as English conjunctive adverbs.

consonant: A consonant is a speech sound that is articulated with complete or partial closure of the vocal tract.

constituency: A syntactic notion that certain groups of words form natural groupings. For instance, the clause The class met in the lab can be traditionally divided on one level into two main constituents: the subject, The class, and the predicate, met in the lab. However, the preposition in and the article the form no natural grouping: in the. Therefore, these two words are not a constituent.

constituent: A constituent is one of two or more grammatical units that enter syntactically or morphologically into a construction at any level.

constituents: Constituent is a word or a group pf words that functions as a single unit.

content word: Nouns, verbs, adjectives, and some adverbs that, unlike function words such as the or very, are fully meaningful.

cooperative principle: The philosopher H. Paul Grice's theory that communication among individuals is cooperative. He proposed various maxims specifying precisely how communication is cooperative. For instance, his maxim of quantity stipulates that what we say should be maximally informative: we should not say too much or too little. If we violate a maxim, a conversational implicature results.

coordinating: The conjunctions and, or, and but that link phrases and clauses.

declarations: A type of speech act that leads to a change in the state of affairs: I now pronounce you husband and wife or I sentence you to 10 years in prison.

declarative sentence: The most common sentence type in English. Declarative sentences contain, minimally, a subject and predicator, with the subject typically preceding the predicator, as in The company went out of business or The teacher dismissed class early.

Glossary

deixis: Deixis is reference by means of an expression whose interpretation is relative to the (usually) extralinguistic context of the utterance, such as: who is speaking; the time or place of speaking; the gestures of the speaker; the current location in the discourse.

demonstrative: The pronouns this, that, these, and those when not used as determinatives.

dental: Refers to sounds made with the tongue touching the teeth.

derivation: Derivation is the formation of a new word or inflectable stem from another word or stem. It typically occurs by the addition of an affix. The derived word is often of a different word class from the original. It may thus take the inflectional affixes of the new word class.

derivational affix: A prefix or suffix added to a word that often changes the meaning of the word (e.g. own in *dis*own) or its part of speech (e.g. rapid [adjective] in rapidly [adverb]).

descriptivist: An individual who is primarily interested in describing objectively the structure of language without interjecting his or her biases about language. Linguists are typically characterized as descriptivists. Compare with prescriptivists.

determinatives: A word class containing words such as a, the, this, some, and every that occupies the first position in a noun phrase: a tiny ant, that tall building, some people.

diachronic: Studying a language from a historical perspective. A diachronic study of English would investigate earlier periods of English, such as Old English or Middle English.

dialect: A variable form of a language. Dialects of a language are considered mutually intelligible. Speakers of Northern American English can understand speakers of Southern American English. However, the notion of mutual intelligibility can be problematic, since the dialects of Chinese (e.g. Mandarin and Cantonese) are not mutually intelligible.

diphthong: A phonetic sequence consisting of a vowel and a glide interpreted as a single vowel; a type of vowel occurring within a single syllable whose quality changes during its articulation. Examples of diphthongs in English include the middle sounds in words such as house /haʊs/ and fight /faɪt/.

direct illocution: A direct illocution is an illocutionary act in which only the illocutionary force and propositional content literally expressed by the lexical items and syntactic form of the utterance are communicated.

direct speech act: A type of speech act in which the speaker's intentions are clearly spelled out. For instance, if a speaker says Clean the house later, his intention is to get someone to do something, since he uses an imperative sentence, a form closely linked with a directive. Compare with indirect speech act.

ejective: A stop made with an aggressive glottalic airstream, such as Hausa [k'].

embedding: A structure occurring within some other structure. In the phrase the leader of the company, of the company is a prepositional phrase occurring within a noun phrase. Therefore, the prepositional phrase is embedded in the noun phrase.

endocentric: An endocentric construction consists of an obligatory head and one or more dependents, whose presence serves to modify the meaning of the head.

exclamatory sentence: A sentence, such as What a lovely day it is or How lovely the weather is that begins with what or how, which is often used for the purpose of emphasis. In writing, exclamatory sentences will typically end with an exclamation mark.

exocentric: An exocentric construction consists of two or more parts, whereby the one or the other of the parts cannot be viewed as providing the bulk of the semantic content of the whole.

experiencer: Experiencer is a person who experiences. (linguistics) A thematic relation where something undergoes a situation or sensation lacking a semantic agent. The subjects of the intransitive verbs *fall* and *burn* are experiencers.

Glossary

explicit speech act: A speech act containing a performative verb, a verb that names the speech act. For instance, the verb *apologize* in *I apologize for being late* marks this speech act as an expressive.

expressive: A type of speech act in which the speaker expresses his or her attitude. An apology is a type of expressive.

figurative language: Figurative language refers to the use of words in a way that deviates from the conventional order and meaning in order to convey a complicated meaning, colourful writing, clarity, or evocative comparison.

finite verb: A finite verb is a verb form that occurs in an independent clause, and is fully inflected according to the inflectional categories marked on verbs in the language.

free morpheme: A free morpheme is a grammatical unit that can occur by itself. However, other morphemes such as affixes can be attached to it.

fricatives: A manner of articulation associated with consonants such as /s/ in sip and /z/ in zip in which the airstream is constricted in the oral cavity, leading to a certain degree of turbulence.

front vowel: Vowel in which the body of the tongue is in the front part of the oral cavity (mouth). The vowels [i, e, ɛ, a] form a set of front reference vowels.

function word: A function word is a word which have no lexical meaning, and whose sole function is to express grammatical relationships. For instance, when the is placed before a noun, as in The office is closed, the marks the noun as definite and specific.

fusional: A language containing a number of inflections that mark such distinctions as case, number, and gender.

General American (GA): A variety of spoken American English that does not associate a speaker with a particular region, social class, or ethnic group in the United States.

generative grammar: Generative grammar is a linguistic theory that regards linguistics as the study of a hypothesised innate grammatical structure.

It is a biological, sociobiological or biologistic modification of structuralist theories, deriving ultimately from glossematics. Generative Grammar considers grammar as a system of rules that generates exactly those combinations of words that form grammatical sentences in a given language.

glottal: An articulation involving the glottis.

glottis: The space between the vocal folds.

grammatical morpheme: A morpheme expressing some kind of grammatical relationship. The article *the*, for instance, indicates that the noun it precedes is definite. The -ed on *parked* marks this verb as being in the past tense.

hard palate: The bony structure that forms the roof of the front part of the mouth.

head: A word which can stand for a phrase on its own is called its head, endocentric phrases are also called headed phrases.

heavy syllable: A syllable containing a tense vowel or ending in a consonant.

hierarchical structure: The manner in which linguistic constructions are grouped. The construction British history teacher is ambiguous because the constructions in this noun phrase can be grouped two ways. If British and history are grouped together, the phrase refers to "a teacher of British history." If history and teacher are grouped, the phrase refers to "a teacher of history who is British.'

homograph: A homograph is a single spelling with two or more meanings. English examples in addition to tear are read, which could be either [rid], the present tense form of read, or [rɛd] the past tense form of read.

homonym: Here are three senses of homonym. A word that has the same pronunciation as another. Homonyms differ from each other in: (1) meaning; origin; usually spelling, (2) Loosely, a homograph, (3) Either of two people with the same name.

homophone: A homophone is a single pronunciation with two or more meanings. English examples in addition to [tu] are [flaʊər], which could be either flower or flour, [sɒlt], [fli], and [sɛnt].

hypernym: A word whose meaning would include the meaning of a more specific word. For instance, the word flower is a hypernym of tulip because the meaning of tulip is included in the meaning of the more general word flower. Compare with hyponym.

hyponym: A word whose meaning is included in the meaning of a more general word. Because a magazine is a type of periodical, magazine would be a hyponym of the more general word periodical. Compare with hypernym. Also see co-hyponyms.

idiom: An idiom is a multiword construction that is a semantic unit whose meaning cannot be deduced from the meanings of its constituents, and has a non-productive syntactic structure.

illocutionary act: A speech act that conveys speaker intentions. The intent of *I"m sorry I'm late* is to issue an apology (a type of expressive) for something the speaker has done wrong.

imperative sentence: A sentence such as *Stop talking* in which the base form of the verb is used, and the subject is an implied you.

implicit speech act: A speech act such as *Shut the door* that does not contain a performative verb.

inflection affix: An inflectional affix is an affix that: (1) expresses a grammatical contrast that is obligatory for its stem's word class in some given grammatical context; (2) does not change the word class of its stem; (3) is typically located farther from its root than a derivational affix; (4) produces a predictable, nonidiosyncratic change of meaning.

inflection: Inflection is variation in the form of a word, typically by means of an affix, that expresses a grammatical contrast which is obligatory for the stem's word class in some given grammatical context. In contrast to derivation, inflection: (1) does not result in a change of word class; (2) usually produces a predictable, nonidiosyncratic change of meaning.

instrument: Instrument is the semantic role of an inanimate thing that an agent uses to implement an event. It is the stimulus or immediate physical cause of an event.

interdental: Articulated with the tongue between the upper and lower teeth. Many speakers of American English use an interdental articulation in words such as *thick, thin*.

intonation: Intonation is the system of levels (rising and falling) and variations in pitch sequences within speech.

IPA: The International Phonetic Alphabet (IPA) is an alphabetic system of phonetic notation based primarily on the Latin script. It was devised by the International Phonetic Association in the late 19th century as a standardized representation of speech sounds in written form.

irony: Irony is a trope in which an expression is used in such a fashion as to convey the opposite meaning of what is expressed.

labiovelar: An articulation involving simultaneous action of the back of the tongue forming a velar closure and the lips forming a bilabial closure.

lexical semantics: The study of the meaning of individual words in a language. A verb that can occur alone or after one or more auxiliaries in the verb phrase. In the verb phrase *may have left*, *left* is the lexical verb. Because lexical verbs are an open class, there are many different lexical verbs in English.

lexicon: A lexicon is the knowledge that a native speaker has about a language. This includes information about: (1) the form and meanings of words and phrases; (2) lexical categorization; (3) the appropriate usage of words and phrases; (4) relationships between words and phrases, and (5) categories of words and phrases. Phonological and grammatical rules are not considered part of the lexicon.

linear structure: How linguistic constructions are ordered relative to one another. For instance, in English adjectives come before the head noun (e.g. *the healthy child*). In contrast, in languages such as French or Spanish, adjectives tend to come after the noun (e.g. French *l'enfant en bonne santé* "the child healthy"). Compare with hierarchical structure.

Glossary

linguistic context: The larger body of words in which linguistic constructions occur, often affecting the use of particular constructions. For instance, old information is often placed at the beginning of a clause, as is the case with He in the second sentence: The man committed a crime. He was arrested.

linguistics: Linguistics is usually defined as "the scientific study of language", it is informed by a long history of the study of grammar, and many of the ideas central to current linguistic theory go back to ancient times.

liquid: A cover term for laterals and various forms of r-sounds.

main clause: A clause that typically contains a subject, predicator (with a finite verb), and no markers of subordination. In *Although we arrived on time, the movie had already started*, the second clause is a main clause that contains a subject (*the movie*), a finite verb (*had*), and no marker of subordination. Because the first clause contains a marker of subordination (*although*), it is not a main clause but a subordinate clause.

manner of articulation: Manner of articulation is the type of closure made by the articulators and the degree of the obstruction of the airstream by those articulators.

metaphor: Here are two senses of metaphor: (1) A metaphor is the expression of an understanding of one concept in terms of another concept, where there is some similarity or correlation between the two; (2) A metaphor is the understanding itself of one concept in terms of another.

metonymy: Here are two senses for metonymy: (1) Metonymy is, broadly defined, a trope in which one entity is used to stand for another associated entity. (2) Metonymy is, more specifically, a replacive relationship that is the basis for a number of conventional metonymic expressions occurring in ordinary language.

minimal pairs: A minimal pair is two words that differ in only one sound./Words that differ by only one sound in the same position (e.g. fit /fɪt/ and kit /kɪt/). Minimal pairs are useful for determining which sounds in a language are phonemes.

mixed metaphor: Mixed metaphors are different metaphors occurring in the same utterance, especially the same sentence, that are used to express the same concept. Mixed metaphors often, but not always, result in a conflict of concepts.

modal auxiliaries: A closed class of auxiliary verbs, including *may, might, can, could, shall, should, will, would*. Modal auxiliaries always occur before primary auxiliaries in the verb phrase: *should have gone*.

modifier: A modifier is a constituent, in an endocentric construction, that imparts information relating to the head of the construction.

monophthong: A vowel, such as /i/ in *keep* or /u/ in *boot*, whose pronunciation remains fairly constant in a syllable. Compare with diphthong.

morpheme: The smallest meaningful unit in language. See also bound, free, derivational, and inflectional morphemes.

morphological typology: Morphological typology is the categorization of a language according to the extent to which words in the language are clearly divisible into individual morphemes.

morphology: Morphology is the study of the internal structure of words. Morphology can be thought of as a system of adjustments in the shapes of words that contribute to adjustments in the way speakers intend their utterances to be interpreted.

nasal: A manner of articulation associated with consonants, such as /m/ in *moon*, during whose articulation the air flows through the nasal cavity.

noun phrase: A phrase having a noun as its head: *the ugly duckling, many small animals that were released into the wild*. A noun phrase generally includes one or more modifying words, but allowance is usually made for single-word minimal noun phrases that are composed only of a noun or pronoun.

nucleus: The nucleus (sometimes called peak) is the central part of the syllable, most commonly a vowel. In addition to a nucleus, a syllable may begin with an onset and end with a coda, but in most languages the only part of a syllable that is mandatory is the nucleus.

Glossary

onset: An onset is the part of the syllable that precedes the vowel of the syllable. "s" is the onset of "*sit*". "*p*" is the onset of "*pie*."

open class: An open class is a grammatical class of words with a potentially unlimited membership. These words have content meaning. (nouns, verbs, adjectives, and adverbs) Compare with closed classes.

patient: A grammatical patient, also called the target or undergoer, is the participant of a situation upon whom an action is carried out or the thematic relation such a participant has with an action. Sometimes, theme and patient are used to mean the same thing.

person deixis: Person deixis is deictic reference to the participant role of a referent, such as: (1) the speaker; (2) the addressee, and (3) referents which are neither speaker nor addressee.

personification: Personification is an ontological metaphor in which a thing or abstraction is represented as a person.

phone: A phone is an unanalyzed sound of a language. It is the smallest identifiable unit found in a stream of speech that is able to be transcribed with an IPA symbol.

phonemes: An individual speech segment that is distinctive and that contrasts with other speech segments. One way to determine phonemes in a language is to look at minimal pairs. The minimal pairs hat and cat indicate that the segments /h/ and /k/ are phonemes in English.

phonetic alphabet: An alphabet used to study speech sounds in which every symbol corresponds to one and only one sound.

phonetics: Phonetics is the study of human speech sounds.

phonology: Phonology is the study of how sounds are organized and used in natural languages.

phonotactic constraints: Constraints on permissible sequences of sounds in a given language. For instance, while English allows the sequence /pl/ at the start of a syllable (as in *play*), it does not allow the sequence */pf/.

phrase: A group of words centered around either a noun, verb, preposition, adjective, or adverb. For instance, very quickly is an adverb phrase centered on the adverb quickly; in the morning is a prepositional phrase centered on the preposition in. See also **head**.

place deixis: Place deixis is deictic reference to a location relative to the location of a participant in the speech event, typically the speaker.

place of articulation: How the articulators—the tongue, teeth, lips, and various parts of the mouth—are involved in the articulation of sounds. For instance, the sounds /p/ and /b/ are bilabial sounds because their articulation involves both lips.

plosives: A manner of articulation involving consonants such as /t/ and /g/ whose pronunciation involves complete blockage of the airstream in the oral cavity followed by release of the air.

politeness: Cultural conventions in a language governing polite levels of speech.

polysemous/polysemy: Words such as bank that have more than one meaning.

pragmatic meaning: Meaning that is determined by context. For instance, the sentence *It's cold in here* could mean not just that the temperature is low (its grammatical meaning) but that the person uttering this sentence requests that the heat be turned up.

pragmatics: The study of principles specifying how language is used. Conventions of politeness, for instance, are dictated by cultural norms having nothing to do with **grammaticality** but rather with conventions for how specific forms should be used. In English, a form such as Could you please help me is a polite form for making a request.

predicate: A predicate is the portion of a clause, excluding the subject, that expresses something about the subject.

predicator: A predicator is the verb in its functional relation to the clause. It is comparable to the grammatical relations of subject and object.

prefixation: Prefixation is a morphological process whereby a bound morpheme is attached to the front of a root or stem. The kind of affix involved in this process is called a prefix.

prescriptivists: People such as teachers, editors, and writers of usage handbooks who tell people how they should use language. See also prescriptive rules.

presupposition: A presupposition is background belief, relating to an utterance, that: (1) must be mutually known or assumed by the speaker and addressee for the utterance to be considered appropriate in context; (2) generally will remain a necessary assumption whether the utterance is placed in the form of an assertion, denial, or question, and (3) can generally be associated with a specific lexical item or grammatical feature (presupposition trigger) in the utterance.

pronoun: A pronoun is a pro-form which functions like a noun and substitutes for a noun or noun phrase.

referential deixis: A type of deixis in which expressions refer to something or someone. For instance, in The computer is broken, the noun phrase The computer refers to a specific computer in the external world.

rime: A rime is the part of a syllable which consists of its vowel and any consonant sounds that come after it. "*It*" is the rime of "*sit*." "*Oil*" is the rime of "*spoil.*"

root: A root is the portion of a word that: (1) is common to a set of derived or inflected forms, if any, when all affixes are removed; (2) is not further analyzable into meaningful elements, being morphologically simple, and (3) carries the principle portion of meaning of the words in which it functions. If a root does not occur by itself in a meaningful way in a language, it is referred to as a bound morpheme.

semantic role: A semantic role is the underlying relationship that a participant has with the main verb in a clause. Semantic role is the actual role a participant plays in some real or imagined situation, apart from the linguistic encoding of those situations.

semantics: Here are two senses for semantics: (1) Semantics is, generally defined, the study of meaning of linguistic expressions. (2) Semantics is, more narrowly defined, the study of the meaning of linguistic expressions apart from consideration of the effect that pragmatic factors, such as the following, have on the meaning of language in use: Features of the context; Conventions of language use; The goals of the speaker.

simile: A simile is a comparison between two things. It is signalled overtly; in English, a simile is expressed by the words like or as.

social deixis: Social deixis is reference to the social characteristics of, or distinctions between, the participants or referents in a speech event.

soft palate: The soft, movable part of the palate at the back of the mouth.

spatial deixis: A type of **deixis** that locates something spatially relative to the speaker in space, as *there* does in the sentence *The book is over there*.

speech acts: Statements of speaker intentions. For instance, the sentence *Leave* is a **directive** whose purpose is to get someone to depart.

statement: Here are two senses for statement: (1) A statement is an illocutionary act that has the assertive illocutionary point of saying that some state of affairs is true. (2) A statement is a sentence having a form that is typically used to express such illocutionary acts (such as an English declarative sentence which has a subject followed by a verb).

stem: A stem is the root or roots of a word, together with any derivational affixes, to which inflectional affixes are added.

stop: Complete closure of two articulators. This term usually implies an oral stop—that is, complete closure of two articulators and a velic closure, as in English [b] in *buy*. But nasals, as in English [m] in *my*, can also be considered stops.

stress: Stress refers to the relative prominence or emphasis of certain syllables in a word; stress is usually produced by an increase in articulatory force, by an increase in the airflow, and sometimes by increased muscular tension in the articulators.

structural metaphor: A structural metaphor is a conventional metaphor in which one concept is understood and expressed in terms of another structured, sharply defined concept.

subject: A cause function realized by a noun phrase or clause. First and third person pronouns have subjective forms, but nouns do not. Subjects typically occur towards the start of a clause, except in yes/no questions, where they switch positions with the operator: *You* are leaving—Are *you* leaving?

suffixation: Suffixation is a morphological process whereby a bound morpheme is attached to the end of a stem. The kind of affix involved in this process is called a suffix.

suprasegmentals: Sounds, such as pitch and sentence stress, occurring in units larger than the individual phoneme.

syllable: A syllable is a unit of sound composed of a central peak of sonority (usually a vowel), and the consonants that cluster around this central peak.

synchronic: Studying a language in its current form. A synchronic study of English would focus on Contemporary English: English as it is spoken and written in the early twenty-first century.

synonymy: A relationship between words that are equivalent in meaning.

temporal deixis: A type of deixis that locates something temporally relative to the speaker. For instance, in the sentence We should leave tomorrow, the adverb tomorrow locates the act of leaving in the future relative to the time this sentence was uttered.

time deixis: Time deixis is reference to time relative to a temporal reference point. Typically, this point is the moment of utterance.

tone: A pitch that conveys part of the meaning of a word. In Chinese, for example, [ma] pronounced with a high level tone means "mother", and with a high falling tone means "scold".

unbound stem: An unbound stem is a stem which can occur by itself as a separate word. Another morpheme need not be affixed to it in order for it to be a word.

universal grammar: Noam Chomsky's notion that there are features of grammar common to all languages. For instance, all languages have first and second person pronouns.

unvoiced: A sound is unvoiced if during its articulation the vocal cords do not vibrate. Sounds such as /p/, /f/, and /s/ are unvoiced.

utterance: A linguistic construction that may not be grammatically well-formed but that nevertheless has meaning and is communicative. For instance, if one person utters *I just won the lottery* and a second person replies *Wow*, the reply has meaning, even though it is not a grammatically formed sentence with a subject and predicator.

velar: The sounds in velar group are made with the tongue near the velum, the soft part of the roof of your mouth, behind the palate.

verb phrase: A phrase consisting of an obligatory lexical verb and optional auxiliary verbs.

voiced: A sound is voiced if during its articulation the vocal cords vibrate. Sounds such as /d/, /v/, and /z/ are voiced.

voiceless vowel: A voiceless vowel is a vowel that is produced with no vibration of the vocal folds.

voicing assimilation: A process whereby a **voiced** or **unvoiced** sound will cause a nearby sound to also be, respectively, voiced or unvoiced. In English, if a noun ends in an unvoiced sound (e.g. /t/ in hat /hæt/), when a plural marker is added, the marker is also unvoiced (e.g. /s/ at end of /hæts/).

vowel: A vowel is a syllabic speech sound pronounced without any stricture in the vocal tract. Vowels are one of the two principal classes of speech sounds, the other being the consonant.

word classes: The particular designations given to individual worlds. The major word classes are noun, verb, adverb, adjective, and preposition.

word formation processes: Processes such as affixation and compounding that lead to the creation of new words.

zero affix: A zero affix is the member of a set of inflectional affixes which is represented by the absence of an expected morpheme.

Answers to Self-Study Activities

Introduction

1. (1) b   (2) c   (3) d   (4) a

2. All languages have rules that specify how constructions are formed, and principles that govern how these constructions are actually used. Rules are tied to competence: the abstract underlying knowledge of a language that any speaker will possess. Principles are tied to performance: how we use the structures that rules create. Thus, if you are studying rules of syntax, you are studying linguistic competence: our knowledge of how we put words together to form phrases and clauses, not our knowledge of how we use these structures once they've been formed.

3. In general, linguists prefer descriptive rather than prescriptive approaches to language study. A descriptivist simply describes language structure, laying out the facts about language X or language Y in objective and scientific terms. A prescriptivist, on the other hand, is more interested in telling people how to use language, often times in very subjective and emotional language (e.g. double negatives are illogical and reflect sloppy thinking).

4. Yes, there are some syntactical differences between Chinese and English. For example, Chinese uses word order instead of articles to distinguish definite nouns from indefinite nouns. Noun phrases that precede the main verb are usually definite or generic, while noun phrases that follow the verb are usually indefinite or generic. Say you have a Chinese sentence that could be glossed as "Cat chase mouse." That would probably be interpreted as "The cat chased a mouse" with the first noun definite and the second noun indefinite rather than the other way around, or as "Cats chase mice," with a gnomic present and both nouns generic. The way to say "The cat chased the mouse"

would be "Mouse, cat chase" (making "mouse" the topic), and the way to say "A cat chased the mouse" would be something like "Mouse, there-is cat, chase" (using an empty existential verb as a placeholder just so that there's something for the noun "cat" to come after).

5. A sentence is grammatical if it is rule governed. Although *China home to the world's highest mountains* is nonstandard, it is rule-governed and thus grammatical. But while this sentence is grammatical, for many people it is unacceptable because of its association with non-standard English. Acceptability involves people's personal judgments of linguistic forms and can be highly subjective.

6. In a system of grammatical gender, gender is somewhat arbitrarily assigned. For instance, in German, das Mädchen ("girl') is assigned neuter gender, even though a girl is biologically feminine. In a system of natural gender, there is a more direct association between biological gender and the assignment of gender. This is why in Modern English, the pronouns he and she always refer to males and females, respectively. There are cases of uses of generic he, as in *An employee must make sure he arrives on time for work*, in which he refers to both males and females. But this usage is dying out in English, and actually sounds a bit archaic to some.

Phonetics

1. A vowel is a sound that needs an open air passage in the mouth. The air passage can be modified in terms of shape with different mouth and tongue shapes producing different vowels. A consonant is formed when the air stream is restricted or stopped at some point between the vocal cords and the lips. We describe each consonant in terms of each of the following: vocing, place of articulation, and manner of articulation. Vowels are determined by three parameters: *height, frontness*, and *roundedness*.

2. /f/ is a voiceless labiodental fricative.   /č/ is a voiceless palatal affricative.
/ŋ/ is a voiced velar nasal.   /n/ is a voiced alveola nasal.
/h/ is a voiceless glottal glide.   /t/ is a voiceless alveolar stop.
/b/ is a voiced bilabial stop.   /r/ is a voiced alveolar liquid.
/g/ is a voiced velar stop.   /m/ is a voiced bilabial nasal.
/š/ is a voiceless palatal fricative.   /θ/ is a voiceless interdental fricative.

3. In a phonetic alphabet, each symbol equals one and only one sound. If the English alphabet became purely phonetic, all speakers of English would simply spell words as they pronounced them, and the current situation—one grapheme often corresponding to many different pronunciations—would cease to exist. However, spelling variation would ultimately increase because pronunciation varies considerably among speakers of English. Thus, a speaker of American English would spell bath differently than a speaker of British English. Thus, we are ultimately better off with the current system, which standardizes (though with some exceptions) how all writers of English should spell words.

4. The words *fast* and *feast* are minimal pairs: words that differ by one phoneme in the same position. Because the substitution of /æ/ for /i/ in this context produces a different word, we know that these sounds contrast and are therefore phonemes.

5. See Table 2.1.

6. Omitted

7. all /ɔːl/
people /ˈpiːpl/
black-eyed /blæk-aɪd/
yellow /ˈjeləʊ/
welcome /ˈwelkəm/

last /lɑːst/
his philosophy /hɪz fɪˈlɒsəfi/
influence /ˈɪnfluəns/
world /wɜːld/
widely /ˈwaɪdli/
help /help/

Phonology

1. Phonetics is the study of sounds in and of themselves. (No reference to any specific language is necessary.); Phonology is the way that a given language treats those sounds. (This REQUIRES reference to specific languages. You cannot study sounds in phonology separated from specific languages.)

2. (1) Gunpowder is another ancient Chinese invention.

(2) The rise and set of sun represents hope in the hearts of Chinese people.

(3) A round moon represents family reunion and often reminds people of their family.

Answers to Self-Study Activities

(4) Characters were carved on each piece of clay which looked like the seals widely used in China.

3. /ˌresɪˈteɪʃn/; /prɪˈdɒmɪneɪt/; /ˌsɪɡəˈret/; /kənˈtest/; /ˈbjʊərəʊ/; /kənˈtentmənt/; /dɪsˈlaɪk/; /ˌʌnkənˈvɪnsɪŋ/

4. (1) Stress can be used in sentences to give special emphasis to a word or to contrast one word with another.

(2) Another major function of stress in English is to indicate the syntactic category of a word.

(3) Stress also has a syntactic function in distinguishing between a compound noun.

5. Omitted

6. Omitted

Morphology

1. (1) Inflectional morphemes can only be suffixes; derivational morphemes can be either prefixes or suffixes.

(2) Inflectional morphemes never change the word class or meaning of a word; derivational morphemes often do change the meaning or word class of a word.

2. non- (bound, derivational), conform (free), -ist (bound, derivational) de- (bound, derivational), context (free), -ual (bound, derivational), -ize (bound, derivational), -ed(bound, inflectional), repeat (free), -ing (bound, inflectional)up (free), on (free)scare (free), -y (bound, derivational, here spelled as -i), -est(bound, inflectional), un- (bound, derivational), test (free), -ed (bound, inflectional), care (free), -less (bound, derivational), -ly (bound, derivational)

3. B 4. D 5. A 6. B 7. B 8. D

9. Omitted

10. The general characters in Chinese usually contain one morpheme while these words contain more than one morphemes. And their meanings are tightly connected with their morphemes. For example, 孬 includes "不" and "好" which means something is not good.

Syntax

1. Syntax is the part of grammar, which investigates the act of producing speech utterances and utterances themselves.

2. Word classes may be classified as open or closed. Open class includes content/lexical words like nouns, most verbs, adjectives and adverbs. In contrast to open class, closed class contains function/grammatical words like auxiliary and modal verbs, pronouns, articles, prepositions, and conjunctions. Open class words deal with content and vocabulary. They have concrete meaning that goes beyond their function in a sentence. These words refer to things, people, actions, description or other ideas that have more than just a grammatical usage. Closed class words deal with the formation of sentences. They have ambiguous meaning and serve to express grammatical relationships with other words within a sentence. They signal the structural relationships that words have to one another and are the glue that holds sentence together. Thus, they serve as important elements to the structure of sentences.

3. In linguistics, the head of a phrase is the word that determines the syntactic type of the phrase. In grammatical analysis, most phrases contain a key word that identifies the type and linguistic features of the phrase; this is known as the head-word or the head.

4. Surface structure is how superficially sentences are closely related, while deep structure is an abstract level of structural organization in which all the elements determining structural interpretation are represented.

5. Omitted

6. Definitions containing wording such as "something expresses "action' or "a state of being'are notional: they attempt to define a category by the particular meanings that constructions in the category express. A formal definition of a verb would focus on, for instance, the morphological or syntactic features that define verbs. For instance, verbs take inflections, such as the various suffixes on likes, liking, and liked.

7. Form deals with the structure of a particular construction. The construction *The weather* is a noun phrase because it contains a noun, weather, as head, and everything else in the noun phrase, the article the, is dependent on the head. However, noun phrases can have many functions in a sentence. In this case, *The weather* is functioning as subject because it occurs before the predicator, has been, and if the sentence were converted into a yes/no question, the operator, has, would change places with the subject: Has the weather been awful lately? The function that a form has is very dependent on its relationship with other forms in a clause.

Answers to Self-Study Activities

8. (1) festival (head of noun phrase); (2) rapidly (adverb phrase); (3) happy (adjective phrase); (4) wished (verb phrase); (5) in (prepositional phrase); (6) farmers (noun phrase)

    9. Omitted;

    10. Omitted;

    11. Omitted;

    12. Omitted

Semantics

1. Semantic fields are classifications of words associated by their meanings. Semantic fields could be clothing, parts of the body, emotions, old boyfriends; the fields may vary across speakers, and words may belong to more than one category.

2. When a symbol, word, or phrase means many different things, that's called polysemy. The verb "get" is a good example of polysemy—it can mean "procure," "become," or "understand.", etc. Generally, polysemy is distinguished from simple homonyms (where words sound alike but have different meanings) by etymology.

3. A metaphor is a figure of speech that describes an object or action in a way that isn't literally true, but helps explain an idea or make a comparison. Here are the basics: a metaphor states that one thing is another thing.

While both similes and metaphors are used to make comparisons, the difference between similes and metaphors comes down to a word. Similes use the words like or as to compare things—"Life is like a box of chocolates." In contrast, metaphors directly state a comparison—"Love is a battlefield."

4. The nouns *bull* and *man* share the features animate and male. However, they are different kinds of animate organisms: a bull would have the feature bovine, a man the feature human.

5. It is difficult to find words that are exactly equivalent in meaning, and that can be substituted one for the other in any context without some change in meaning. For instance, the words *hate* and *abhor* both express extreme dislike of something or someone. However, while I hate spinach and I abhor spinach both express this dislike, abhor seems somewhat odd in this context: one abhors violence, but not food.

    6. (1) b (2) c (3) a (4) b (5) c (6) a

7. Omitted

Pragmatics

1. (1) ambiguous words, phrases, and sentences, (2) deictics, (3) figures of speech, (4) indirect illocution, and (5) presupposition. Examples are omitted.

2. (1) a   (2) c   (3) d   (4) b   (5) e

3. A discussion of the grammatical meaning of *I wouldn't mind another glass of wine* would focus on the meaning of the words and structures in this statement. For instance, *I* refers to the speaker; *another glass of wine* works together as a unit of meaning specifying an additional serving of a specific type of alcoholic beverage placed in a drinking vessel typically used to hold this beverage; the expression *wouldn't mind* conveys the meaning that the speaker has no objections to drinking more wine. To determine the pragmatic meaning of the statement, it is necessary to place it in some social context, such as a small get-together among friends. In this context, one could imagine the host asking the speaker whether he or she wanted *another glass of wine*, and the speaker replying with an indirect speech act for reasons of politeness. If the speaker made the statement without any prompting, it would be interpreted as somewhat impolite because he or she is being a bit too insistent.

4. Grammatically well-formed sentences: (i) I really like chocolate ice cream; (ii) My second favourite flavour is vanilla; (iii) I don't care for vanilla; (iv) I think it has great taste

Utterances (i.e. incomplete sentences that are meaningful but lack a subject and predicator):

(i) Me too; (ii) Too tasteless, in my opinion; (iii) Really

5. (1) Direct. An imperative sentence that is a directive: the speaker directly tells someone to do something. (2) Indirect. This is a "hint": a very indirect suggestion that the addressee shut the door to prevent further mosquitoes from getting into the house. (3) Direct. A declarative sentence that is a commissive: the speaker is directly committing himself to doing something in the future. (4) Indirect. An interrogative sentence that is a directive: the guest is not interested in knowing whether someone at the table is physically able to give her the butter. She's using a conventionalized yes/no question to politely request that someone give her the butter.

6. Hazel has violated the maxim of relation: her sudden discussion of

the weather has nothing to do with Fred's gossip about Christine. But Hazel's violation of this maxim is purposeful, and Fred's likely interpretation of her utterance (i.e., the conversational implicature of her violation) is that Hazel is uncomfortable with his gossiping about Christine, or that she is trying to warn him that they should shift topics so that Christine doesn't hear their gossip.

(1) The conventions of formal written English first of all stipulate that writers adhere to the maxim of quantity: they must fully develop the topics they introduce, while at the same time not saying too much so they are not perceived as "padding" their papers. Second, writers must follow the maxim of relation: everything they write must be related and relevant to the topic at hand; digression, or going off topic, is not tolerated. Third, writers must observe the maxim of quality: everything they write must be truthful. There are cases where scientists have gotten into serious trouble for fabricating the results of their experiments. Finally, writers must adhere to the maxim of manner: clarity of expression is of utmost importance in formal written English.

(2) In the first turn, the library patron is adhering linguistically to the generosity maxim. In his statements, he expresses the efforts he has exerted to return the missing newspapers to the library. However, instead of simply thanking him, the library worker engages in a serious violation of the tact maxim: he does not "maximize benefit" to the library patron, but very indirectly issues a directive in an attempt to get the patron to do the worker's job for him. In the final turn, the library patron arguably violates the tact maxim too, but given the library worker's violation of this maxim, the patron's anger is justified.

7. Omitted

8. Omitted

9. 在汉语中，身份不同，对"我"的表达完全不一样。皇上用朕、孤，皇后用本宫、臣妾，皇太后用哀家，百姓用鄙人、草民。老人用老夫，青年用小生，和尚用贫僧，道士用贫道。尼姑用贫尼，神仙用本神，本仙君。豪放的说洒家，婉约的说不才。

Bibliography

Aarts, B., & McMahon, A. (Eds.). (2008). *The handbook of English linguistics*. John Wiley & Sons.

Allan, K. (2014). *Linguistic meaning (RLE Linguistics A: General Linguistics)*. Routledge.

Anderson, C. (2018). *Essentials of linguistics*. Mcmaster University Press.

Ashby, M., & Maidment, J. (2005). *Introducing phonetic science*. Cambridge University Press.

Austin, J. L. (1975). *How to do things with words* (Vol. 88). Oxford university press.

Bauer, L., & Laurie, B. (1983). English word-formation. Cambridge university press.

Biber, D., (2010). *Longman student grammar of spoken and written English*. Pearson Education.

Blyth, C. & Sykes, J. (2020). Technology-enhanced L2 instructional pragmatics. *Language Learning & Technology, 24*(2), 1–7.

Brown, P. (2020). *Politeness*. The International Encyclopaedia of Linguistic Anthropology, 1-8.

Burdina, S. V. (2013). *Theoretical Grammar: method, guides for students of higher educational institutions*. State Institution Luhansk Taras Shevchenko National University Press.

Chierchia, G., & McConnell-Ginet, S. (2000). *Meaning and grammar: An introduction to semantics*. MIT press.

Coulmas, F. (Ed.). (1997). *The handbook of sociolinguistics*. Oxford: Blackwell.

De Marchena, A., & Eigsti, I. M. (2016). The art of common ground: Emergence of a complex pragmatic language skill in adolescents with autism spectrum disorders. *Journal of child language, 43*(1), 43.

Dellwo, V., Huckvale, M., & Ashby, M. (2007). How is individuality expressed in voice? an introduction to speech production and description for speaker classification. *Speaker Classification*. Springer-Verlag.

Denham, K., & Lobeck, A. (2012). *Linguistics for everyone: An introduction*. Cengage Learning.

Frawley, W. (2013). *Linguistic semantics*. Routledge.

Giegerich, H. J. (1992). *English phonology: An introduction*. Cambridge University Press.

Greenbaum, S. (1996). *The Oxford English grammar* (Vol. 652). Oxford University Press.

Grice, P. (1989). *Studies in the way of words*. Harvard University Press.

Bibliography

Halliday, M., Matthiessen, C. M., & Matthiessen, C. (2014). *An introduction to functional grammar*. Routledge.

Hartsuiker, R. J., & Bernolet, S. (2017). The development of shared syntax in second language learning. *Bilingualism*, 20(2), 219.

Hayakawa, S. I. (1967). Language in thought and action. *The Florida English Journal, 3*(2), 1-12.

Herbst, T. (2010). *English linguistics: A coursebook for students of English*. Walter de Gruyter.

Hofmann, T. R. (2015). *Realms of meaning: An introduction to semantics*. Routledge.

Huddleston, R., & Pullum, G. K. (2005). *A student's introduction to English grammar*. Cambridge University Press.

Hurford, J. R., Heasley, B., & Smith, M. B. (2007). *Semantics: A coursebook*. Cambridge university press.

Katz, J. J. (1965). The relevance of linguistics to philosophy. *The Journal of Philosophy, 62*(20), 590-602.

Kempson, R. M. (1977). *Semantic theory*. Cambridge University Press.

Kreidler, C. W. (1998). *Introducing English semantics*. Psychology Press.

Kwong, C. (2009). Translating classical Chinese poetry into rhymed English: a linguistic-aesthetic view. *TTR: Traduction, terminologie, rédaction, 22*(1), 189-220.

Ladefoged, P., & Johnson, K. (2014). *A course in phonetics*. Nelson Education.

Leech, G. N. (2016). Principles of pragmatics. Routledge.

Levinson, S. C. (1983). *Pragmatics: Cambridge textbooks in linguistics*. Cambridge University Press.

Levinson, S. C., Brown, P., Levinson, S. C., & Levinson, S. C. (1987). *Politeness: Some universals in language usage (Vol. 4)*. Cambridge: Cambridge university press.

Marshall, C. R., & van der Lely, H. K. (2012). Irregular past tense forms in English: how data from children with specific language impairment contribute to models of morphology. *Morphology, 22*(1), 121-141.

Mathews, P. H. (1974). *Morphology: An introduction to the theory of word-structure. Cambridge textbooks in linguistics*. Cambridge.

McWhorter, J. H. (2008). *Understanding linguistics: The science of language*. Teaching Company.

Meyer, C. F. (2009). *Introducing English linguistics*. Cambridge University Press.

Miller, G. A. (1998). *WordNet: An electronic lexical database*. MIT press.

Murphy, M. L. (2003). *Semantic relations and the lexicon: Antonymy, synonymy and other paradigms*. Cambridge University Press.

N. Richard. (2020). Hierarchy in grammar. Retrieved from ThoughtCo thoughtco.com/hierarchy-syntax-term-1690835.

Ogden, R. (2017). *Introduction to English Phonetics*. Edinburgh University press.

Papi, M. B. (2010). How does pragmatics fit with the brain? New challenges from complex systems theories. *Italian Journal of Linguistics, 22*(1), 209-228.

Peña, E. D., Bedore, L. M., Lugo-Neris, M. J., & Albudoor, N. (2020). Identifying developmental language disorder in school age bilinguals: Semantics, grammar, and narratives. *Language Assessment Quarterly*, 1-18.

Pinker, S. (2003). *The language instinct: How the mind creates language.* Penguin UK.

Quirk, R. (2010). *A comprehensive grammar of the English language.* Pearson Education.

Robins, R. H. (2013). *A short history of linguistics.* Routledge.

Sampson, G. (2005). *The Language instinct debate.* A&C Black.

Searle, J. R. (1985). *Expression and meaning: Studies in the theory of speech acts.* Cambridge University Press.

Stockwell, R., & Minkova, D. (2001). *English words: History and structure.* Cambridge University Press.

Tench, P. (2015). *The intonation systems of English.* Bloomsbury Publishing.

Todd, L. (2000). *An introduction to linguistic.* Longman Publishing Group.

Wierzbicka, A. (1996). *Semantics: Primes and universals.* Oxford University Press, UK.

Wilson, D. (1979). *Introduction to contemporary linguistic semantics.* Prentice Hall.

Yonggang, Z. H. A. O. (2018). Theoretical studies on the interaction at syntax-phonology interface and chinese prosodic hierarchy. *Journal of Beijing International Studies University, 40*(2), 23-44.

塞缪尔·早川, 艾伦·早川, Samuel Hayakawa, & Alan Hayakawa. (2015). 语言学的邀请. 北京大学出版社.

李倩. (2015). 回锅肉和香菇菜心的语言等级. 商务印书馆.